Opera Guide 35

Alberich and the three Rhinemaidens at Covent Garden in 1964 (photo: Donald Southern)

Foreword

To 'wallow in the highlights' is one way of hearing Wagner; but a greater understanding and appreciation of the form, structure and harmony of the music, as well as a true realisation of the intimate and subtle relation between music and text, can be obtained by a reading of these Guides.

Reginald Goodall   *November 20, 1985*

35

The Rhinegold/
Das Rheingold

Richard Wagner

Opera Guide Series Editor: Nicholas John

Published in association with
English National Opera and The Royal Opera

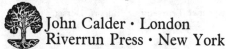
John Calder · London
Riverrun Press · New York

First published in Great Britain, 1985 by
John Calder (Publishers) Ltd.,
18 Brewer Street,
London W1R 4AS

First published in the U.S.A., 1985 by
Riverrun Press Inc.,
1170 Broadway,
New York, NY 10001

BRITISH LIBRARY CATALOGUING IN PUBLICATION DATA

Wagner, Richard, *1813-1883*
    [Rheingold. English] The Rhinegold = Das Rheingold. — (English National Opera
    guides; 35)
    1. Wagner: Richard, *1813-1883*. Rheingold
    I. [Das Rheingold. *English*]   II. Title
    III. Porter, Andrew   IV. English National Opera   V. Royal Opera   VI
    Series
    782.1'092'4   ML410.W1A29

ISBN 0-7145-4078-1

AMERICAN LIBRARY OF CONGRESS CATALOG NUMBER: 85-52161

Typeset in Plantin by Margaret Spooner Typesetting, Bridport, Dorset
Printed by Camelot Press Ltd, Southampton

Contents

List of Illustrations

The Beginnings of 'The Ring'

John Deathridge

The size of Wagner's greatness will always be disputed. But no one can deny that he wrote, at least in terms of length, the biggest work in the history of Western music: *The Ring of the Nibelung*. He also left what may be the largest number of sketches and autographs for any single work of art. Almost 800 manuscript pages of text and 3,750 of music include drafts of two preliminary essays, three short prose sketches, four detailed prose drafts, twelve verse drafts, six full-length composition drafts, three first drafts of the full score (*Rhinegold, Valkyrie, Siegfried* Acts One and Two), and four autograph scores, two of which (*Rhinegold* and *Valkyrie*) were in the possession of Adolf Hitler at the end of the Second World War and are now lost.

Yet despite this wealth of documentation the story of how Wagner began to write *The Ring* is still unclear. Wagner himself is surprisingly reticent about it. There is no equivalent of the stormy sea voyage via Norway to London in 1839 that inspired *The Flying Dutchman* or the sight of the historic Wartburg in Thuringia on the way back to Germany from Paris in 1842 that is supposed to have stimulated the composition of *Tannhäuser*. Nor do the literary complements of these powerful autobiographical images have any parallel in the history of *The Ring*. If Heinrich Heine's version of the Dutchman story gave Wagner the idea of redemption as an effective resolution of tragic conflict and C.T.L. Lucas's paper on the Wartburg song contest opened a 'new world' of operatic possibilities taken from the German Middle Ages, no such central significance is attached to any of the *Ring* sources. Wagner speaks of a plan contemplated 'with reserve'. He says nothing about exactly when, why, or how he came to conceive the project before 1848. All he is prepared to reveal is that by 1848, when he first wrote down his ideas for *The Ring*, he had already been considering an opera based on the Siegfried legend 'for quite a long time'.

Wagner's virtual silence about the beginnings of *The Ring* is perhaps both shyness and a way of heightening his own claim to originality by soft-pedalling the popularity of the subject in Germany at the time. If few except Wagner had seen operatic possibilities in the Dutchman or Tannhäuser material, many were aware of the theatrical potential of the Nibelungen myth and remained eager to adapt it even when it was widely known that Wagner would eventually produce a version that would count as his *summum opus*. Raupach wrote a play *Der Nibelungenhort* based on the myth (*The Nibelungs' Hoard*) as early as 1828 and published it in 1834. According to Ernest Newman, Mendelssohn was inspired by his sister Fanny with enthusiasm for a Nibelungen opera in 1840, but soon abandoned the idea. Henrich Dorn's five-act opera *Die Nibelungen* (*The Nibelungs*) was produced by Liszt in Weimar in 1854 with Wagner's niece Johanna in the role of Brünnhilde — an event that must have tarnished Liszt's early support of the *Ring* project in Wagner's eyes, especially as Dorn was an old rival. Wagner's negative remarks in his autobiography about the Austrian dramatist Friedrich Hebbel, too, are not unconnected with feelings of rivalry with the latter's successful Nibelungen plays written in the late 1850s.

As early as 1844 the philosopher Friedrich Theodor Vischer published an influential essay, *Vorschlag zu einer Oper* (*Suggestion for an Opera*) suggesting the Nibelungen as the subject of a new kind of dramatic work he called a 'grand heroic opera'. Vischer's ideas were replete with criticisms of Romanticism and politically suggestive phrases about the *Vaterland* and the innate Germanness of the Nibelungen heroes, so it is hardly surprising that Wagner is supposed to have been 'almost certainly' (Ernest Newman) acquainted with them. Attempts have also been made to prove that he knew Vischer's disciple Louise Otto and her libretto *Die Nibelungen* — a 'grand heroic opera' in five acts written in 1846 and published in 1852 when Robert Schumann showed some interest in setting it. Yet there is no concrete evidence that Wagner knew the work of either Vischer or Otto. If he did know about their proposed Nibelungen operas, any fears he may have had about the originality of his own project were unfounded. Vischer did not accept that a Nibelungen opera could be written by a composer with symphonic ambitions — an opinion that would hardly have endeared him to Wagner in the 1840s when the idea of symphonic opera was already beginning to take hold in a work like *Lohengrin*. And Wagner's combination of German and Scandinavian sources in *The Ring* alone developed the material far beyond what Vischer and Otto had managed to do with the German epic poem *Das Nibelungenlied*, the only source they seriously considered. Wagner's assertion in a letter to Liszt (November 20, 1851) was fully justified: when the first plan for *The Ring* was written down in 1848, he had regarded it from that moment on as his own 'poetic property'.

*   *   *

The earliest evidence of Wagner's intention of turning the Nibelungen myth into an opera does not originate with Wagner himself but with another source. On April 1, 1848, Eduard Devrient, an actor and director at the Dresden Court Theatre where Wagner was employed in the 1840s as Royal Kapellmeister, wrote in his diary: 'He [Wagner] tells me about a new plan for an opera based on the Siegfried legend.' Since the diaries show that Devrient and Wagner met regularly to discuss art and politics, the description of the plan as 'new' suggests that Wagner had developed it only shortly before the meeting on April 1 took place. According to his autobiographical writings, he had the idea directly after he had attempted to write *Friedrich I*, a spoken drama on the subject of Friedrich Barbarossa. This is confirmed by Cosima Wagner's diaries in which Wagner is quoted as saying (November 12, 1871): 'I am glad that I have an eye for this connection between legend and history . . . the compilation of the Nibelung Saga . . . began with Friedrich I.'

In describing the gestation of *The Ring* in the months leading up to the Dresden Revolution of May 1849 Wagner presents his interest in history and myth as a fundamental aesthetic and intellectual confrontation. A variety of sources, however, show that the final choice of myth as the true source of the new revolutionary opera was not quite as straightforward as Wagner later claimed. There is no doubt that he wrote down a prose draft embracing the substance of the entire *Ring* from the theft of the Rhinegold and the building of Valhalla to the deaths of Siegfried and Brünnhilde. The draft was called *Die Nibelungensage (Mythus)* and was completed on October 4, 1848. From this condensed presentation Wagner crystallised the plot of *Siegfried's Death* (later entitled *Twilight of the Gods*), completing the first verse libretto by November 28, 1848. But the clean autobiographical image of a final confrontation with German political history in the shape of Friedrich Barbarossa leading inexorably to the 'purely human' world of myth in

Siegfried's Death from which Wagner never looked back is complicated by, among other things, an entry in Devrient's diaries strongly suggesting the reverse. On February 22, 1849, *i.e.* almost three months after the completion of *Siegfried's Death*, Devrient wrote: 'Kapellmeister Wagner read a historical-philosophical essay in which, with extraordinarily intelligent and poetic synthesis, he developed the uplifting enthuasiasm for world domination from the earliest sources of the legends. Friedrich I emerged as the most powerful embodiment of this idea — a figure of gigantic, wonderful beauty. He [Wagner] wants to turn Friedrich into a drama.'

Contrary to Wagner's account and most biographers who have repeated it, he seems to have lost interest in *The Ring* immediately before and after the Dresden Revolution. Besides *Friedrich I*, he wrote extensive drafts for a number of other theatrical projects, including two operas *Jesus von Nazareth* and *Wieland der Schmied*. He toyed with the idea of creating a drama about Achilles. And in the years after the Revolution and his flight from Dresden to Switzerland he spent much time seeking a commission from the Paris Opéra and writing several theoretical treatises. Not surprisingly, then, he found little time for *Siegfried's Death* although he never abandoned it completely. And when he did find time to sketch some music for it in July/August 1850, encouraged by Liszt's offer of a prospective performance in Weimar, he soon put it aside again — this time for different reasons.

The *Ring* project began to leave operatic reality for more utopian realms soon after the première of *Lohengrin* under Liszt's direction in Weimar in August 1850 — a performance about which Wagner heard nothing but negative reports from friends who had managed to hear and see it. On September 14, 1850, Wagner wrote to E.B. Kietz that he was still thinking of setting *Siegfried's Death* to music, but not of having it performed by any institution that just happened to be interested in it. The letter to Kietz is something of a historic document since it contains the first mention of the festival idea that played a major role in the conception of *The Ring* as we know it today. 'Here [in Zürich] I would design and build a theatre made of wood,' he told Kietz, 'invite the most suitable singers, and organise everything necessary for a special event so that I could be sure of an excellent performance of the opera [*Siegfried's Death*]. Then I would invite everyone interested in my works, make sure that the auditorium is filled properly, and give three performances in a week — gratis of course — after which the theatre would be pulled down and the whole thing would be over for good.'

A few months after writing to Kietz, Wagner announced to Theodor Uhlig in a letter dated May 10, 1851, that he had been plagued for 'the entire winter' with an idea for an opera on the story of the youth who sets out into the world 'to learn what fear is' and who is stupid enough 'never to want to learn'. Wagner told Uhlig that this would become *Der junge Siegfried (The Young Siegfried)* — later entitled *Siegfried*, and that he would start composing it as soon as he had finished the libretto. But the composition of the new opera, like *Siegfried's Death*, failed to materialise, although, again like *Siegfried's Death*, some sketches for it survive. In another letter to Uhlig written between October 6 and 12, 1851, Wagner announced this time that he had 'big ideas' about Siegfried: 'three dramas with an introduction in three acts'. He then wrote prose sketches for *Der Raub des Rheingoldes (The Theft of the Rhinegold)* and *Siegmund und Sieglinde: der Walküre Bestrafung (Siegmund and Sieglinde: the Punishment of the Valkyrie)* and completed the librettos of what became *The Rhinegold* and *The Valkyrie* in the following year. Strictly

9

'The Rhinegold' at Bayreuth in 1897: (left) Friedrichs and Breuer as Alberich and Mime and (right) Elmblad as Fafner, Weed as Freia and Ernst Wachter as Fasolt (Royal Opera House Archives)

speaking, Wagner was not creating anything new since he was simply expanding, step by step, the concept outlined in 1848 in *Die Nibelungensage* (*Mythus*). But in technique and emphasis, not to mention social function, the project was changing rapidly. What had begun as a 'grand heroic opera' turned into two 'dramas' and was becoming a trilogy with introduction that was eventually given the generic title 'Stage Festival Play'. Technically speaking, certain narrative elements in *Siegfried's Death* and *The Young Siegfried* were now redundant. Parts of the story that were simply related by characters on stage in these two works had themselves become part of the action in *The Rhinegold* and *The Valkyrie*. The significance of this in terms of Wagner's ideas about leitmotif has been the subject of much ingenious, though unprovable, speculation since sketches documenting the musical beginnings of *The Ring* are surprisingly scarce.[1] What is certain is that the fine tuning of the entire project involved not only the redistribution of its narrative structure, but also a redressing of dramatic balance due to two significant additions to the beginning and the end of the cycle. On November 18, 1852, Wagner wrote to Uhlig: 'At the moment I am working on *The Young Siegfried* and should soon be finished with it. Then I have to start on *Siegfried's Death* — that's going to take longer; two scenes have to be completely rewritten (the

[1] See *e.g.* Carl Dahlhaus, 'Zur Geschichte der Leitmotivtechnik bei Wagner' *Das Drama Richard Wagners als musikalisches Kunstwerk*, Regensburg 1970, p. 34f. According to Dahlhaus, the mythical elements in the *Ring* concept had a paradoxical musical significance. On the one hand, the mere narrative exposition of the myth in *Siegfrieds Tod* provided a barrier for the leitmotivic technique which, according to Wagner's treatise *Opera and Drama* (1850-51), was the musical means of actualising the complex world of myth in scenic terms. On the other hand, the recapitulation of the myth in the enlarged conception of *The Ring* became the reason for rich motivic expansion which intensifies as the work proceeds. What had originally impeded Wagner's musical imagination thus came to stimulate some of his most powerful music.

10

Norns' scene and Brünnhilde's scene with the Valkyries [Waltraute in the final version]) and above all the ending.'

* * *

In view of the period in which *The Ring* was first conceived, it is hardly surprising that the first version of its ending contained in the 1848 draft *Die Nibelungensage* (*Mythus*) is meant to symbolize the banishment of an old social order and the restoration of the monarchy which, divested of its feudal interests, should continue its rule of the republican state. The king, highest symbol of the old order, was to become, cleansed of the guilt of his social class, the highest power of the new. Wagner turned this somewhat contradictory political idea into a grandiose choral finale at the end of *Siegfried's Death*. Brünnhilde enters a flaming pyre with Siegfried's body in order to extinguish the curse and to purify the ring that is returned to the Rhinemaidens — or Wasserfrauen (waterwomen), as they are called in this version — and transformed again into the Rhinegold from which it was forged. Brünnhilde declares that Wotan is all-powerful and everlasting, and the chorus supports this triumphantly. Alberich appears behind Hagen and orders the latter to save the ring. Suddenly a dazzlingly bright light shines out of the flames in which Brünnhilde, with helmet and gleaming armour, rides through the air on a shining horse leading Siegfried by the hand. The Rhine breaks its banks and the Wasserfrauen carry away the ring and the tarnhelm. They pull down Hagen with them and Alberich sinks down 'with a woeful gesture'. Thus Wotan, god of the old law, retains his natural power after Siegfried and Brünnhilde have sacrificed their lives for the banishment of the curse and the emergence of a kingdom of freedom.

The uncomfortable political metaphor was also aesthetically awkward. The choral restoration of the gods (reminiscent of Greek tragedy), the melodramatic intrusion of Alberich and Hagen and the picture-postcard pink of the romantic image of Brünnhilde and Siegfried (reminiscent of the ending of *The Flying Dutchman*) simply did not mix. After expanding *The Ring* in 1851 and 1852, Wagner gave the cycle a radically new ending which replaces the original choral scene announcing the restoration of Wotan with a monologue by Brünnhilde who, sounding as if she has just finished reading the complete works of Ludwig Feuerbach, defines the new social order as the emergence of 'love' (*Liebe*) in antithesis to 'law' (*Gesetz*). She then proclaims the opposite to what she had said in the first version of the ending: the downfall of the gods. The burning of Valhalla now symbolized the dissolution of the law of the gods and as a political allegory, almost four years after the Dresden Revolution, it actually brought Wagner closer to, and not further from, the ideas of his former comrade-in-arms, the Russian anarchist Michael Bakunin.

In the past the question of exactly when Wagner decided to change the ending of *The Ring* has been clouded by the assumption that there is a direct correlation between Wagner's aesthetic strategies on the one hand, and the political consequences of the 1848/1849 Revolution on the other. Kurt Hildebrandt, for instance, states specifically in a famous book on Wagner and Nietzsche (1924) that December 2, 1851 — the day of Louis Napoleon's *coup d'état* in Paris — 'meant for Wagner not only the day of political resignation, but also — even if he still wasn't completely aware of it — the negation of the world.' Bernard Shaw, too, in a chapter entitled 'Why He Changed His Mind' added to the first German edition of *The Perfect Wagnerite*, saw Wagner's decision to change the emphasis of *The Ring* from the heroic Siegfried to the tragic resignation of Wotan, and with it the ending of the whole work, as a

Eva Turner as Freia in 1924 at La Scala (Royal Opera House Archives)

realistic reaction to the failure of the Revolution and the establishment of the forces of reaction. Yet Ernest Newman had little trouble in pointing out that the prose draft of *The Young Siegfried* written down in May 1851, *i.e.* seven months before Louis Napoleon's victory, already contains the phrase 'the end of the gods'. Close analysis of other sources, too, suggests that Wagner made the decision even earlier than this, possibly before the Dresden Revolution.[2]

Apart from anything else, the new ending of 1852 — *pace* Hildebrandt and Shaw — was actually more radical than the one it had replaced. Yet its moral implications, and the obvious discrepancy between the purification of the ring synonymous with the rescue of the gods on the one hand and the downfall of the gods on the other, did not seem to disturb Wagner. Furthermore, he had introduced another new element in the 1851/1852 version of *The Ring* that is not to be found in the initial plan of 1848: Alberich's curse on love. This, the focal point of the opening scene, was now the complement of the new ending. The contrast between lovelessness and love went hand in hand with that between the fear that grows out of lovelessness, and the fearlessness that guarantees love. Thus if Siegfried's fearlessness in *Siegfried* could be seen as a

[2] See W.A. Ellis, 'Die verschiedenen Fassungen von "Siegfrieds Tod", *Die Musik*, i. (1901-2), 751, 879; and Ernest Newman, *Wagner Nights*, London 1949, p. 440f. For a different interpretation, see Carl Dahlhaus, 'Über den Schluss der "Götterdämmerung"', *Wagner — Werk und Wirkung*, Regensburg 1971, 97-115; and yet another, John Deathridge, 'The Ending of the "Ring"', publication forthcoming.

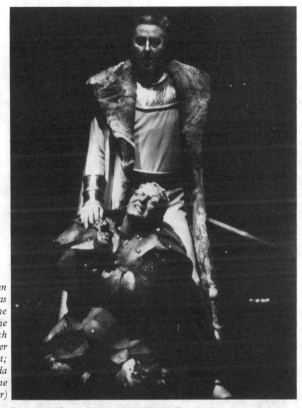

Leif Roar as Wotan and Wolf Hirte as Alberich at the Bayerische Staatsoper, Munich in 1975; producer Günther Rennert; designer, Jan Brazda (photo: Sabine Toepffer)

reverse reflection of Wotan's fear of the end in *The Valkyrie*, the curse on love for the sake of power at the beginning of the cycle became a distorted mirror image of the dissolution of power for the sake of love at the end, and Brünnhilde's message to the survivors of the gods' catastrophe a direct antithesis of Alberich's curse. The moral dialectic of this arrangement, contained as it is within a rather rigid system of opposites, accounts for the seeming permanence of the ambiguities of *The Ring*. But there is no doubt, too, that it caused Wagner a great deal of heartache about the ending. Hildebrandt's and Shaw's claim that Wagner's *volte-face* was a reaction to the outcome of the 1848/1849 Revolution was not about the new ending of 1852, but really an interpretation of other, much later attempts to alter the ending again in the spirit of Schopenhauer and Buddhist philosophy. At the last minute Wagner found a solution that contained only remnants of his attitude to the revolutionary politics of 1848/1849 and had less to do with either Feuerbach, Schopenhauer or Buddha than is generally thought.[3] Nevertheless, the contradictions brought about by the involved beginnings of *The Ring* were an artistically fruitful flaw which, in the end, even Wagner's genius nearly failed to conquer. On November 25, 1880, Cosima Wagner noted in her diary: '[Richard] takes a look at the ending of *Twilight of the Gods* and says that he would never do anything as complicated as this ever again.'

[3] For details of the dramatic symmetries of *The Ring*, and for radically different interpretation of the ending, see Dahlhaus 'Über den Schluss...' & Deathridge, *op cit.*

(Below) a contemporary drawing of the machinery used at Bayreuth in 1876 to simulate the Rhinemaidens swimming and (above) a scene from Tony Palmer's film 'Wagner' showing the machinery in action.

'The Rhinegold' — The Music

Roger North

The Prelude and Scene One

By its nature, a prelude consisting of 136 bars of the note E flat and its major chord proclaims the beginning of something vast — not just the four-scene, two-and-a-half hour *Rhinegold*, but the whole four-opera, fifteen-hour *Ring*. It proclaims also Wagner's return to musical composition after five fallow years, during which his mind, consciously and unconsciously, was searching in the histories of both music and drama, and putting together an entirely new sort of continuous operatic libretto, which would demand an entirely new and continuous musical treatment. The provider of this continuity would be the

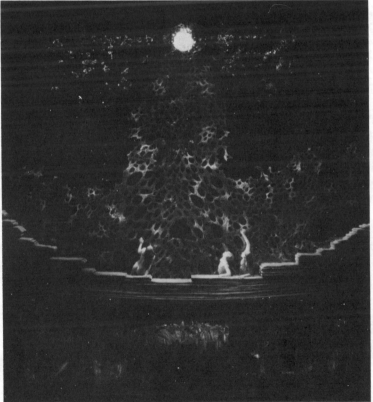

The Rhinemaidens glory in their gold at Bayreuth in Peter Hall's production, designed by William Dudley, in 1984 (photo: Festspielleitung Bayreuth)

orchestra. In his own words: '. . . the *orchestra* [Wagner's italics] . . . takes an unbroken share, supporting and elucidating on every hand: it is the moving matrix of the music . . .'[1] He had also found his own true musical self for, in

[1] Wagner, *Opera and Drama* (trans. Ellis) Vol II, p. 338.

15

spite of almost exclusively composing operas, Wagner's real musical father was the primarily instrumental Beethoven. So *The Rhinegold* prelude ushers in a new operatic era too, for no composer would be unaffected.

The *Ring* preludes are scene-setters, not the highly seminal symphonic opening statements of *Tristan*, *Mastersingers* and *Parsifal*. Wagner had yet to be influenced by Liszt in this respect. Nevertheless the opening horn motif [1a], given out 32 times, latterly densely overlapping and needing all of eight horns, will, in addition to its immediate progeny, [1b] and [1c], give birth to several later motifs containing the upward arpeggio figure ending on the third of the chord (*e.g.* [23]).

We are, or will be when the curtain rises, at the bottom of the Rhine. The music suggests the primeval world at rest, unraped by greedy, power-seeking man. 'Calm', says the score. A gently swirling watery figure climbs up through the strings and subsides. Its skeleton [1b] goes with it in the bassoons. Its movement doubles [1c] (stems up), as the more discernible clarinets (stems down) enliven [1b]. Although the whole orchestra except percussion and trumpets is used for most of the prelude, the music should remain quiet and calm throughout, merely surging a few times just before it is sharply cut off for the voices to enter. The result of the cut is that we wait for the prelude music to return and carry on, as it soon does, thus firmly establishing the orchestra's predominance. The first Rhinemaiden's opening pentatonic melody [2] will have offspring, among them the song of another child of nature, the woodbird in *Siegfried* [53c] and the 'sleep' motif of Brünnhilde in *The Valkyrie* [43]. The swirling watery music continues in the strings, now also matching the Rhinemaidens' swimming.

A momentary slip into a minor key (the first key change) marks Flosshilde's warning that they do not guard the gold well with their games, and only a moment later Alberich is there, the key more continuously minor and the swirling music now largely chromatic. On the wet rocks Alberich slithers, and the music with him.

This becomes his motif, the convulsive slide representing his violence and malevolence on other occasions, *e.g.* [22]. His four-note down-scale vocal figure is clearly a variant. Alberich has come for love. The Rhinemaidens egg him on in turn, each providing a musical episode and each concluding with the refrain of their dissonant laughter.

The third and most melodious of these, Flosshilde's, which is accompanied by throbbing sensuous chords, particularly enraptures Alberich, who is therefore particularly pained by the laughter we now perceive to be present all along in the pulsating chords. In his agony he utters a figure, reflecting and slightly altering one of Flosshilde's, itself similarly reflecting an earlier one.

FLOSSHILDE Wie deine An-muth mein Aug'__ er – freut

378

Oh, how your beauty de - lights my eyes

FLOSSHILDE dei - nen ste-chen-den Blick, deinen strup-pi-gen Bart

390

Oh, the sting of your glance, and the prick of your beard

ALBERICH Die dri - tte so traut, be - trog sie mich auch?

414

The third one, so dear, be – trays me as well?

Here we see in operation Wagner's art of transition, of which he was proud. Alberich's first phrase (bracketed), which has thus evolved, will turn out to be one of the most important motifs in *The Ring* and will be associated with love and its goddess, Freia [11b]. Here it is in its minor, unrequited form.

The Rhinemaidens' opening music returns to round off this section. The orchestra has indeed been the moving matrix. [1c] (stems down) has returned three times and the swirling figure has never been absent for long. Alberich now chases the maidens in furious lust, while the orchestra develops his and their themes in alternation. As he finally gives up exhausted, the sun strikes down through the water and lights up the gold. Shimmering strings accompany the simple major arpeggio figure [3]. More important is the Rhinemaidens' joyful cry of 'Rhinegold!' in C major (the new home key), since its minor form will be the cry of misery of those enslaved by what the gold will become [5x].

Alberich and the Rhinemaidens on the hydro-electric dam in the Patrice Chéreau production at Bayreuth, designed by Richard Peduzzi with costumes by Jacques Schmidt, 1980 (photo: Festspielleitung Bayreuth)

17

A major-to-minor change produces the ring motif [6], as Wellgunde unwisely spills the beans to Alberich, but the all-powerful ring can only be forged by one who forswears love, sings Woglinde to the solemn C minor [7a]: 'Nur wer der Minne / Macht versagt.'

The end of the scene now approaches. The orchestra returns, but not in its original key, to the scene-opening [2] and then to the Rhinemaidens' [4y] rejoicings. The orchestra recapitulates the rest of [4], running straight on into the music which bred and now rebreeds the 'ring' motif. Alberich takes this up, wondering for a moment if he can cunningly get joy without love, and carries the music to C minor (in which the scene will end) and to an orchestral restatement of Woglinde's 'Nur wer der Minne . . .'. His mind is soon made up. To the maidens' cries of joy now distorted into screams of horror, he clambers up to the gold whose motif [3] sounds despairingly in the minor to be echoed, further distorted, and followed by a blaring 'ring' motif [6]. Alberich curses love, then grabs the gold and makes off, plunging the whole scene into darkness. Furious C minor swirlings are punctuated for a while by the helpless cries of the Rhinemaidens and Alberich's mocking laughter, then left alone to rise and fall as 'the whole stage is filled from top to bottom with black, swirling water.' The prelude's 136 bars of Eb harmony are matched here by a mere 26 of two very slowly alternating C minor harmonies, but there are 42 bars of C minor swirlings. As they die away to be later vaporised into clouds, we hear once again, this time mournfully on cor anglais and horn accompanied by the sombre Wagner tubas, Woglinde's 'Nur wer der Minne / Macht versagt.' The orchestra in effect speaks Woglinde's words and Wagner's remembrance-motif technique speaks for itself.

Wagner's new operatic method has worked splendidly in this first scene, but it has not been so very difficult for him. He has been able to maintain the swirling music virtually throughout — a procedure hardly different from, say, Schubert's *Gretchen am Spinnrade* — matching the balletic swimming of the Rhinemaidens and occasionally contrasting with the similarly matched slitherings and scramblings of Alberich, this contrast especially exploited in the short development just before the revelation of the gold. The trio of Rhinemaidens has provided the formal quality of ensemble, coalescing into a homophonic mini-chorus at important moments. Thus fusing elements of ensemble and ballet, Wagner has composed an opening number which is not all that revolutionary. The real test will come in scene two and Wagner will not get full marks.

The swirling music disappears into the watery depths of the cellos underneath the memory of Woglinde's 'Nur wer . . .' [7a] to reappear in the misty heights of violins, flutes and harp in alternation with the memory of Alberich's 'The world's wealth can be mine', the last words sung to the 'ring' motif [6], which gradually warms up from cor anglais and clarinets, through bassoons, violas and horns, and transforms itself into the first phrase, [8a and b] of Wotan's 'fortress of Valhalla' theme on Wagner tubas and trumpets, which follows to start scene two.

Scene Two

Valhalla with gleaming battlements stands high above us, gradually coming into view as the day dawns. The only real transformation needed to turn [6] into [8ab] is that of minor to major and of thin parallel thirds to rich hymnlike full harmony. Fricka's words will explain the dramatic connection. Wotan built the fortress, she says, to gain more dominion and power . . . for these

Wotan (James Morris) and the newly-built Valhalla, San Francisco, 1985 (photo: William Acheson)

worthless playthings would he blasphemously gamble away love and woman's worth? This last phrase is set to Woglinde's [7a] in the orchestra and partly sung by Fricka. The payment to the giants for building the fortress is to be Freia, the love-goddess. Future modification of the 'ring' motif must carefully avoid invoking 'Valhalla' unless that is intended. The converse problem is easily and usually solved by using the latter's second phrase:

Wotan and Fricka are asleep during the opening statement of the 'Valhalla' theme which, after some dialogue between them, is recapitulated in full, Wotan this time joining in, singing an occasional phrase or part-phrase of the melody but mainly his own harmonising part. In future this will be a common procedure of Wagner's, but for most of the ensuing dialogue he has to fall back on conventional recitative which the orchestra 'supports' harmonically. It only 'elucidates' spasmodically — with a low and rather vague, descending scale when the contracted payment is being discussed, with the 'ring' motif and other fragments of the 'Valhalla' motif at other times. Two short arioso moments are provided by a sentimental melody [10] with words about a comfy home to restrain Wotan's wanderlust. It contains the falling seventh, so often associated in *The Ring* cycle with a loving woman (*cf.* [40], [65], [72]) and will be used by the crafty Loge later on.

To [11] in the violins Freia rushes on. Wagner's motifs must, of course, express the emotion of the moment, and so the love-goddess's [11b] sounds

Robert Tear as Loge and Yvonne Minton as Fricka in the Götz Friedrich production at Covent Garden, designed by Josef Svoboda with costumes by Ingrid Rosell, 1980 (photo: Reg Wilson)

rather different from the love-sick, spurned Alberich's 'the third one, so dear' of scene one (see p. 17) which it expands. Soon to the heavy tread of the appropriately crude [12] hammered out on timpani, brass and strings, the giants, Fafner and Fasolt, appear to collect their fee. But Wotan repudiates the deal and Fasolt's speechless amazement at this is accompanied by the descending scale now clearly crystallised into [9a]. Fasolt cites the Runes of Covenant carved on Wotan's spear and a moment later, on the top line of the trite little canonic [15] (an offspring of [9a]) lectures Wotan on keeping his word, the cellos and basses in complete agreement (*i.e.* having the same thing to say) on the bottom line. To an orchestral stream of motifs Fasolt contrasts the gods, who rule through beauty [11a] yet want a castle ('Valhalla', second phrase) for which they will forfeit the wondrousness of woman [7a], with the giants' clumsiness and toil [12] to win 'a woman gentle and fair to grace our poor dwelling' [11]. Fasolt joins in on [7a], which is fragmentary, and [11], which here is fair and gentle in the major and on an oboe. Fafner, however, is a power man and only wants Freia because she tends the golden apples which keep the gods immortal. A nature-type pentatonic motif for these, [16a] is rhythmically and melodically akin to the prelude and the Rhinemaidens' music [1 and 2]. Without Freia's apples the gods will become sick and pale — to which words we hear [16b] on cor anglais and bassoon — and waste away.

The giants move to take Freia but her brothers, Froh and Donner, try to prevent this until, to [9a] fortissimo on trombones, Wotan interposes his spear between them and the giants. 'Force will not serve! This bond is graved on my spear's strong shaft', he says. In the nick of time the devious Loge now arrives, anxiously awaited since he has promised Wotan to get him out of the contract. A flamboyant character, we too welcome him among this bickering crowd of seemingly ungodlike gods, and there is a musical welcome as well. The orchestra has been busy stating the dramatically relevant motifs, but this is not enough. Since the opening 'Valhalla' 'aria' for tubas and then trumpets, recapitulated after a short digression as a duet for tubas with Wotan, there has been no formal musical piece, and Wagner has not succeeded in avoiding the imbalance of drama and music acceptable in the recitative of traditional 'number' opera, where it would at once be redressed by an aria or ensemble. As fire-god, several bits of pyro-music ([13] and [14] are some) go with Loge, related in varying degrees to each other. The alternative of [13a] best expresses his slippery guile and has already appeared (much slower, of course) in Wotan's and Fafner's voice parts in reference to Loge's craftiness and Wotan's cheating. Loge's figures alternate with each other and then with [8ab], before the orchestra recapitulates in its original key (but on horns with concluding oboe) the whole 'Valhalla' theme as Loge, who is merely playing for time, reports on his inspection of the castle.

George Shirley as Loge and Donald McIntyre as Wotan at Covent Garden (photo: Donald Southern)

After more alternations of his fiery figures Loge eventually, in something approaching but never quite becoming an aria, tells of his search through the world for a substitute for 'woman's beauty and love' — this phrase to a recurring refrain, [7b]. His music incorporates Freia's [11a] and then, as Loge tells of the only living being he found willing to renounce love for gold, Wagner is able to restate in the orchestra most of the scene one themes, [3, 4, 2, 6], with the swirling music in amongst them. The Rhinemaidens' 'Rhinegold' cry [4x] is in a joyless minor at first, but reverts to its original form as Loge ends the first part of his narrative amid general approval of his conveying to Wotan the Rhinemaidens' appeal for restoration of the gold. Manipulating his audience's greed and desires in the second part of his narrative, Loge tells, as Wellgunde did (her music now in the orchestra reforging the 'ring' motif), how an all-powerful ring could be made etc.. In answer to Fricka he craftily points out — singing the 'domestic bliss' melody [10] — the husband-holding power of fine jewellery, which the ring would keep dwarves busy forging (the first appearance of the important hammering [17], offspring of [4y]). The condition that the would-be ring-forger must renounce love Loge discloses only now, at the end of his narrative, which brings him round formally to the subject of its start. He does this to [7a], singing most of it, and then, singing his refrain [7b], tells us that Alberich has made the ring.

Loge's music has provided a timely cohesiveness. A coda to his narrative is developmental, the dramatic situation allowing free interplay of most of its motifs. All now fear Alberich and want the ring, except Loge who suggests they steal it but return it to the Rhinemaidens. Fafner even convinces Fasolt that the ring would be preferable to Freia.

To a modified, less seismic form of the giants' tramping [12], Fafner announces that instead of Freia they will accept Alberich's gold, and they will hold her until the gods get it. So Freia, to an expansion of the latter end of [12] without the dotted rhythm, is dragged unhappily off. Mournful versions of Freia's [11] are heard against a nebulous background of tremolando strings, and the gods suddenly grow old, grey and weak. [16a] in the minor and Loge, who sings the words '(How) grey you've grown' to [16b], provide the answer — without Freia, there will be no more rejuvenating golden apples. That settles it for Wotan. He and Loge will go to Nibelheim and get the gold. They slip through a crevice in the rock but not before Loge has, for the sixth and last time in this scene, and to Wotan's annoyance, put in a word for the Rhinemaidens whose 'Rhinegold' cry [4x] is heard here sadly in the woodwind.

We now embark on the first of Wagner's great orchestral journeys in *The Ring*, which are as psychological as they are geographical. All-pervading sulphurous vapours on stage call forth matching music, among it some of Loge's figures, of which [13a] alternates in development with his refrain [7b]. I will now call the latter, which carries complex feelings about Alberich having forsworn the love of woman, the 'renunciation cadence'. It starts (as does also its second bar) with the long-short falling step of [4x], a despairing and accelerating form of which follows on its own, to be quickly transformed into reiterations of Alberich's 'the third one, so dear' (see p. 17). These climb until the motif of the gold [3] is heard in the minor, followed at once by the plunging thirds of the 'ring' motif [4]. The rhythm of the 'spurned' Alberich figure needs very little alteration to become that of the hammering [17], which now ferociously accompanies [3] joined to a fortissimo, long drawn out,

The journey down to Nibelheim in Götz Friedrich's production, designed by Peter Sykora, at the Deutsche Oper, Berlin, 1984 (photo: Kranichphoto)

immensely mournful [11b] (Freia's musical connection with the unloved Alberich now clear) on trumpets, and then dying away on a trombone as we hear the approaching sound of hammer on anvil in the rhythm of [17]. The scherzo of the *Rhinegold* symphony is now well under way, owing not a little to that of Beethoven's Ninth, especially the three-bar rhythm section. There are supposed to be eighteen anvils backstage. The unforgettable sound swells, then dies as the strings of the orchestra take up [17] again, this time in conjunction with a drawn out [4x] low in the bass but reiterated as it rises. [17] rises too, finally plunging down the 'ring' motif's thirds as before, and we are there, having beaten Wotan and Loge to Nibelheim by several minutes.

Scene Three
Alberich's orchestral motif opens the scene as he drags his brother Mime by the ear from a side-passage. His vocal variant comes on his words 'You will be pinched' (see p. 16). Mime has failed to conceal and use for himself the magic, invisible-making helmet he manufactured for Alberich. Wagner's 'Tarnhelm' motif [18] is magical in every way. Its second, unexpectedly minor, chord from a remote key-region gives an unnatural or supernatural quality, while its pianissimo muted horns and final bare fifths call from the dark depths of the traditional German Romantic forest. Alberich, invisible, chastises Mime to the demi-semi-quaver slides of his motif, then delivers a terrible sermon of ruthless, sadistic, absolute power to all the Nibelungs, his vocal variant now turned up-scale and leading to imperious falling octaves with, towards the end, a 'ring' motif in the background. As he goes off to torture the other

Alberich (Walter Berry) forces the Nibelungs to amass more treasure for him, San Francisco, 1985 (photo: William Acheson)

Nibelungs we hear the motif of their toil combined with two forms of the Rhinegold 'cry', which now clearly represent *their* cries and shrieks of agony.

Wotan and Loge appear and Mime to [19] (harmonic thirds like those of the 'ring' motif but plunging more deeply in pairs) tells of his predicament, then to [17] without the cry, how the dwarves were once happy smiths working for themselves, but now... *etc.*. The cry rejoins [17], which has firmly established itself as the main theme of the first part of the scene. We really arrived in Nibelheim when we heard it in the orchestral journey cum scene-link — the anvils still ring in our ears — whose music from then on is being recapitulated now as Mime tells his tale. The cry is succeeded as before by the thirds of the 'ring' motif plunging down to Alberich's slides, which started the scene. Even the 'Tarnhelm' motif [18] is set against [17] as Mime whines on about that.

To [17], plus the cry, Alberich returns with a whip, driving a treasure-laden team of Nibelungs. Tormenting them and Mime, he restates musically some of his terrible sermon, and the first half of the scene comes to an imposing end with a demonstration of their terror of the ring when Alberich takes it from his finger and holds it up. The 'ring' motif [6], quiet and quite low, is followed by a devastating transformation of the Rhinemaidens' [4x] and [4y] into [5], wherein [x] on woodwind with a brass and percussion staccato attack on the first chord of each pair diminishes each time from *forte* to *piano*, while [y] loudens from *piano* to *fortissimo* on the heavy brass with cymbal and tam-tam. The tam-tam swells on the final chord and only dies away gradually as the terrified, screaming dwarves scatter in all directions. The additional cadence of the last two chords gives Alberich's 'Obey the ring's great lord!' a frightful finality. The musical connection between [4y] and [17] has also been made clear.

In the second half of the scene Loge comes to the fore. His alternative [13a],

Malcolm Rivers as Alberich at the Seattle Opera Wagner Festival in 1975

25

modified with an element of [14] and scintillatingly orchestrated, punctuates his manipulation of Alberich.

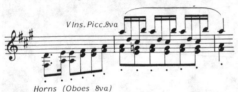

In an almost lilting three-in-a-bar Loge flatters, maintaining the menace of [17] with 'Erlking' triplets, Alberich boasts of his treasure. With this we hear [20] whose three rising notes come directly from Alberich's terrifying cadence (the end of [5]), itself issuing from the three rising notes of the motif of both sets of Alberich's victims, the Rhinemaidens [4y] and the Nibelungs [17]. Various motifs pass by in the orchestra as Alberich boasts that like him all who live will forswear love for gold [7a and b]. Even the gods in their heavenly heights — reiterated bits of 'Valhalla' [8] now soft and blissful — should beware when the treasure rises from the depths [20].

For Loge's reply, in which he greatly inflates the flattery, imputing godlike qualities to Alberich, the 'Valhalla' theme's second phrase hurriedly prefixes Loge's modified figure. Cleverly he induces Alberich to demonstrate the power of the Tarnhelm. Its motif [18] is followed by [21] on the bass tubas as Alberich becomes a serpent of which Loge pretends to be terrified, and then by different music as Alberich becomes a toad which Loge and Wotan seize. A triumphant 'Valhalla/Loge' sounds as they drag Alberich off.

All the second half of the scene has been carried along in an orchestral matrix which, except for the rather intrusive 'serpent' music, has been continuously three-in-a-bar, slowing a little for the 'Valhalla' theme and the 'Tarnhelm' motif, but colouring all, even Alberich's music, with some of the geniality of its beginning, which accompanied Loge's flattery. The orchestral journey down to Nibelheim was also in three, but a three dominated by the menacing rhythm of [17].

The journey up again in general retraces the musical steps, but does more. The plunging thirds of the 'ring' motif — last before, first now — are comparatively congenial, if steadily becoming less so. The 'renunciation' cadence [7b] arrives early, but the smithy is in position, providing a brief return to the 'scherzo' music after the 'trio'. Like the journey down, this scene-link becomes latterly the next scene's prelude. The metre changes to a treading (but for a little while surging) four-in-a-bar for a symphonic development using fragments of the giants' [12], and 'Valhalla' and Loge's [13a]. [12] combines with the cry and then [13a] sinuously with the aging gods' [16b], and Freia's golden apples [16a in the minor]. This is the music of the end of scene two, and Loge's orchestral figures occur where his words were before. [16a]'s initial falling step becomes a development of the cry [4x] (see p. 22) which leads quickly to some brilliant fiery Loge figures and returns after them in a different form as Wotan and Loge bring Alberich up out of the crevice down which they disappeared at the end of scene two.

26

The ENO production by Glen Byam Shaw and John Blatchley, with Emile Belcourt
(Loge), Derek Hammond-Stroud (Alberich), Norman Bailey (Wotan), Katherine Pring
(Fricka), Dennis Wicks (Fafner), John Tomlinson (Fasolt), Philip Joll (Donner), Henry
Howell (Froh) and Anne Conoley (Freia) (photos: Anthony Crickmay; Mike Humphrey)

Scene Four

The recitative of the opening dialogue in which Wotan and Loge demand a ransom from Alberich is borne along in the treading tempo and metre set up in the orchestral scene-link. As Alberich reflects to himself that with the ring he can get more gold, we hear — Alberich singing the upper notes — the 'ring' motif's last three rising notes [6] become those of the increasing hoard [20], revealing another musical connection. Then the thirds plunge deeper and become [19], henceforth associated with Alberich's or Mime's scheming. So Alberich agrees and whispers an order into his now 'walkie-talkie' ring, whereupon, to an impressive orchestral passage, preceded and concluded with the music of Alberich's earlier demonstration of the ring's terrible power [5], the Nibelungs bring up the hoard. Against a continuous [17], back in its original key, are heard simultaneously the hoard's [20] and the cry, the music growing as the treasure is piled up.

The matrix falters a little under the ensuing dialogue, but there is powerful music to come. Alberich jibs violently at parting with the ring but Wotan forcibly takes it from him; the motif of Wotan's spear, the symbol of his power under the law [9a], ironically precedes this unlawful act, for Wotan intends to keep the ring — his joy in it shows in the orchestra as he puts it on his finger, but the first bar of 'Valhalla' [8a] is followed by the second bar of the 'ring' [6].

Alberich is untied and his convulsive slides become [22], which perfectly expresses his deep resentment. A sneering *sforzato* stopped horn on the C sharp and the clarinets sourly reiterate the *whole* diminished chord, not just two notes of it. After six [22]s Alberich sings [23], equally expressive with nothing under it but a (nevertheless vitally important) timpani roll on F#. The rising part of [23] is the 'ring' motif in reverse. 'Since a curse gained it for me, / my curse lies on this ring!', sings Alberich. Out of [22], [23], the 'ring' motif itself and the cry as in [5x], Wagner constructs one of the most terrible diatribes in music. After delivering it Alberich storms off to [5x] and a modified [17].

In absolute contrast the start of the second part of the scene is sweetness and light — high, blue-sky violins darkened only a little by the steady tread of the approaching giants. Horns and woodwind in a round fatten themselves on Freia's 'golden apples' tune (now back in the major). Other relevant motifs accompany the negotiations for her return to the gods. Fasolt regretfully sings the 'renunciation' cadence [7b]. The piling up of the treasure to hide Freia from him takes place to the trite canon [15] of scene two, now given added substance and meaning by an interweave of [17]. [20], the motif of the rising hoard, follows, but not treated as a fourth musical strand as the post-*Mastersingers* Wagner would have done.

With all the treasure piled up, a plaintive Freia still peeps through a chink ([11] on the oboe) and Fafner calls for the ring to be added; Loge yet again, to their original cry in the orchestra, appeals for its return to the Rhinemaidens. But Wotan will not yield it to anyone. General consternation on stage and a development of the 'ring' motif and the cry in the orchestra are interrupted by the half-emergence of Erda from the rock and her ponderous motif [24] on tuba and bassoons. This is clearly a minor version of [1b]. Interestingly, however, it appears from Wagner's sketches that he thought of [24] first and later applied *its* major form to the concept of primeval nature, finally altering [1a] to be [1b]'s progenitor.[2]

Erda is indeed primeval, senior in most ways to Wotan. She knows all, and

[2] See Westernhagen — *The Forging of the Ring*, Cambridge 1976.

The Nibelungs heap gold around Freia in Joachim Herz's 1973 production, designed by Rudolf Heinrich, in Leipzig (photo: Helga Wallmüller)

to the music of Alberich's resentment [22] and the cry [5x] she warns of great danger. Then, as her motif rises and turns back on itself (this is not easily heard on strings inside a thick woodwind chord) [24, 25], she speaks of a darker day dawning for the gods. The ring should be shunned. With that she sinks back into the rock. A slight musical anticlimax here — Wotan must defer to Erda. To a trumpet fanfare as weak as he is at this moment he brandishes his spear, whose motif [9a] blasting forth on trombones gives him some strength. Singing the 'renunciation' cadence [7b] and throwing the ring on the pile, he welcomes back Freia and the gods' youth. For their rejoicing a melody is concocted out of bright major versions of Freia's [11a] and the aging gods' [16b].

To motifs connected with Alberich, a quarrel between the giants over the sharing of the treasure culminates in Fafner's murder of Fasolt, whereupon the trombones solemnly declaim the terrible music to which only minutes ago Alberich cursed the ring [23]. Wotan makes sure we get the point. He is worried and fearful and must go down to Erda for advice (a veiled reference to [24] in the strings). He has paid for the building with bad money ('Valhalla' [8a] turns easily into the 'ring' [6] with the latter half of Alberich's curse [23] appropriately attached) but Fricka has enticed him to enjoy domestic bliss there ([10] on clarinet), so he has little choice but to enter.

In spite of its predominant orchestra and its third scene scherzo the four-scene *Rhinegold* is not a four-movement symphony. Its two more musically cohesive scenes, the first and third, are nevertheless open-ended, with only brief, different-key backward reference to their starting music. Such recapitulation of this as there is, occurs in other scenes. The music has run continuously and the instrumental structure demanded by the orchestra's predominance must now as a whole be brought to a symphonic conclusion.

Donner summons an orchestral thunderstorm, with the strings in up to nineteen parts and himself leading the various brass in [26]. Some of this will be used to start the next opera. Six harps and Froh join in to help build an ensuing rainbow out of twenty bars of G♭ major harmony, recalling the many more of E♭ in the prelude, whose earliest swirlings are also recalled in a very much slower melody based upon them. As Froh finishes the orchestra begins a complete and expanded recapitulation of 'Valhalla' [8], the opera's most extensive theme, which will, with interpolations, run to the end. In due course Wotan joins in, as he did in the early morning of scene two. Alongside his thirteen-word summary of the day's events the orchestra gives out the motif of 'the ring' and a fragment of Erda's music [24], which prepares the way for the musically-related [27] blazoned forth on the trumpet as Wotan is seized by a Great Idea. Like the fortress, which he salutes with a sword, the Idea will land him in a lot of trouble; but without it there would be no more operas in *The Ring*.

Fasolt lies dead as Wotan points the way to Valhalla in Peter Hall's production at Bayreuth, designed by William Dudley, 1984 (photo: Festspielleitung Bayreuth)

The 'Valhalla' theme resumes shortly, interspersed with 'Loge' figures as he verbally distances himself from the other gods and their folly. In a longer episode, the Rhinemaidens are heard below in the valley mourning the loss of their gold [4b]. The poignant momentary C minor harmony of their cry is followed by a new and extended continuation, more beautiful than any of their scene one music, to which it is an appropriate coda. A harp swirls with them. Wotan can only swear at them, but they have the last word: comfort and truth lie only with them in the depths; false and cowardly are those rejoicing aloft. So, although the 'Valhalla' theme and the Great Idea finally share their common grand cadence, and the fifteen bars of D♭ major harmony (recalling the prelude) restates the music of the rainbow bridge, which the gods cross to Valhalla as the curtain falls, all this musical splendour is, to say the least, questioned. Three huge operas later, as the *Twilight of the Gods* approaches its end, the 'Valhalla' scene will again strike majestically along, but the castle itself will be in flames, and a totally different sort of music soaring above it with the flight of a bird and expressive of love, will at last prevail.

The Language and Sources of 'The Ring'

Stewart Spencer

Kapellmeister Wagner read me his completed opera poem 'Siegfried's Death'. The fellow's a poet through and through. A beautiful piece of work. Alliteration, as used by him, is a real find for opera poems; it ought to be raised to the level of a general principle. There were a number of changes I was able to put to him. I consider this poem to be his best and his most dramatic. Afterwards we spoke at length about language, instruction of the people, Christian development and of course we got on to the state, at which point he again mounted his favourite hobby-horse, the destruction of capital. But there's no doubt his is the most original mind of all the people I know in Dresden.

(Eduard Devrient, diary entry for December 2, 1848)

Reviewing the first Bayreuth performance of *The Rhinegold* in 1876, the Viennese critic Daniel Spitzer commented as follows on the opening moments of Scene One: 'One of the Rhine-daughters, Woglinde, swims to the surface and, with a delightful wriggling movement, circles around a rocky ledge in the centre of the stage, while at the same time emitting a series of natural sounds, "Weia! Waga! Wagalaweia! Wallala weiala weia!"; these sounds have been devised by the Master himself and have achieved great notoriety, but since they have never before been put to use, we are uncertain what frame of mind they are in fact intended to express. The cry of "Weia!" seems to indicate a very disagreeable sensation, the call of "Wallala!", on the other hand, a particularly agreeable one, so that the two together may be intended to characterise the feeling of alternating pleasure and displeasure experienced on immersing oneself in a cold bath.'

The opening lines of *The Rhinegold* had aroused amusement and incomprehension ever since the first public performance of the work in 1869, resulting in the whole of Wagner's *œuvre* being dubbed 'Wigalaweia-Musik'. The composer was moved to defend his neologist gambit in an open letter to Friedrich Nietzsche dated June 12, 1872:

From my studies of J. Grimm I once borrowed an Old German word 'Heilawac' and, in order to make it more adaptable to my own purposes, reformed it as 'Weiawaga' (a form which we may still recognise today in the word 'Weihwasser' [holy water]; from this I passed to the cognate linguistic roots 'wogen' [to surge] and 'wiegen' [to rock], finally to 'wellen' [to billow] and 'wallen' [to seethe], and in this way I constructed a radically syllabic melody for my watermaidens to sing, on an analogy with the 'Eia popeia' [hushabye] of our children's nursery songs.

In other words, the Rhinemaidens' vocalisation is an expression of the sanctity of nature and the childlike innocence of the river's nymphean daughters. It must have pained and puzzled Wagner to find himself so misunderstood, since a belief in the emotional accessibility of both text and music had been central to the aesthetic thinking behind *The Ring*: the right *sound*, in phonological and musical terms, ought to evoke a spontaneous resonance in the listener without any need for the intermediary of rational

31

Katherine Pring as Fricka and Raimund Herincx as Wotan at ENO (photo: John Garner)

Donald McIntyre as Wotan, Yvonne Minton as Fricka and Joan Carlyle as Freia at Covent Garden (photo: Donald Southern)

thought processes. Here, too, lies the justification for Wagner's use of early Germanic metre as the verse-form of *The Ring*, a form which he believed (quite rightly) reproduced the natural speech-rhythms of the age of heroes. As he expresses it in *A Communication to My Friends*:

At the archetypally mythic source where I found the youthful and handsome human being, Siegfried, I also found, quite involuntarily, the sentiently consummate linguistic expression in which this man alone could manifest himself. This was *alliterative verse*, which, in keeping with true speech inflections, can be adapted to suit the most natural and lively rhythms; which is at all times readily capable of the most infinitely varied expression; and in which the folk themselves once wrote poetry at a time when they were still poets and the creators of myths.

This credulous belief in the poetic abilities of the *Volksseele* was an essential article of Romantic faith and derives ultimately from Viconian thought: the common people, being closest to nature, spoke the language of the heart. By recreating that language, Wagner hoped to address a direct emotional appeal to the stultified hearts of his nineteenth-century listeners, and arouse in them a sense of the human emotions which he felt had been destroyed by the corrupting influences of modern civilisation. Or, as he puts it in *Opera and Drama*:

Just as we had to remove from the content of the drama all external distortions, all that has to do with the pragmatism of history, with the stage and with dogmatic religious belief, in order to depict that content as something purely human and instinctively necessary, so we must now exclude from its linguistic expression all that derives from these distortions of the purely human and of instinctive necessity and all that corresponds to these alone, and we must remove these features in such a way that only its kernel remains.

By removing all unnecessary 'noise' (in the modern linguistic sense) and by compressing the number of weighted syllables in each line of verse, Wagner aimed at producing an emotionally charged language in which the number of heavily accented syllables, linked together by initial rhyme, would vary according to the intensity of the feelings that were being expressed. By a process of somewhat circular reasoning, Wagner has here arrived back at a definition of Old Norse metres as embodied in the Poetic Edda. In doing so, he paid an unacknowledged debt to Ludwig Ettmüller[1], whose influence on the verse-form of *The Ring* cannot be overestimated. Alone among early nineteenth-century Germanists, Ettmüller realised that Old Norse metrical forms were not related to those of Greece and Rome, and that nothing was to be gained by totting up the number of syllables in each line of verse. Instead,

1 Ludwig Ettmüller (1802-1877) had published an edition of the *Voluspá* in 1830 but far more important from Wagner's point of view was his *Lieder der Edda von den Nibelungen. Stabreimende Verdeutschung nebst Erläuterungen* (Zurich 1837). The crucial influence of this edition was noted by Hermann Wiessner in *Der Stabreimvers in Richard Wagners 'Ring des Nibelungen'* (Berlin 1924). Wiessner's analysis of the poem of *The Ring* suggests that personal contact with Ettmüller in Zurich in the early 1850s helped Wagner to refine his understanding of Eddaic verse-forms, with the result that metrical irregularities in *Siegfried's Death* were removed from the text when it was revised as *Twilight of the Gods* at the end of 1852.

Wotan leads the gods up to Valhalla in the Welsh National Opera production by Göran Järvefelt, designed by Carl Friedrich Oberle (photo: Catherine Ashmore)

Ettmüller analysed the lines in terms of *Hebungen* and *Senkungen* or lifts and dips (also called sinkings), noting that there were typically two, occasionally three, lifts per line, with a variable number of dips dividing them. In the following example, taken from Ettmüller's rendering of the *Fáfnismál*, the crosses indicate the lifts; alliterating staves are underlined:

Dá liegt Rĕgin,	There lies Regin,[2]
sinnt Răth bei sĭch;	confers with himself;
will trügen, der ihm	plans to deceive the man
trăute, den Mănn;	who trusts him;
aus Nĕid er dĕnkt	out of envy he thinks
auf nĭchtige Händel;	of deeds of destruction:
der Fălschhărt will	the false one plans
Făfnirn rächen.	to avenge Fafnir.

2 *i.e.* Wagner's Mime. Regin is Fafnir's brother, hence the reference to revenge in the final lines. My English translation makes no attempt to reproduce the verse-form of the original.

The strophic form here is that of *fornyrdislag* in which each line (technically described as a half-line) consists of two lifts and a varying number of weak and unstressed syllables. The lines are linked together alliteratively in pairs; the main stave or *hofudstafr* is located on the first lift of the second half-line, while the two lifts in the first half-line are treated as supporting staves or *studlar*, one or both of which must alliterate with the main stave. For the purposes of alliteration, all vowels and diphthongs may rhyme with each other. Moreover, since Wagner's native Saxon dialect does not distinguish between voiced and voiceless stops, we occasionally find the characters lapsing into Leipzig regionalisms:

Dort die Kröte,	There, the toad!
greife sie räsch!	Capture it quick!

A second Eddaic verse-form is that of the so-called *ljódaháttr* in which two half-lines are followed by an independent full line with (usually) three lifts, at least two of which must alliterate: viz:

Häuptes kürzer lass' er	Shorter by a head
den haarigen Schwätzer	let the shaggy-haired prattler
fahren hin zur Hel;	wend his way to Hel;
ihm dann eigen	then all the gold
wird alles Gold,	shall be his own,
der Hort, den Fafnir hegte.	the hoard that Fafnir harboured.

The two verse-forms, *fornyrdislag* and *ljódaháttr*, may coexist within a single lay, as we may see from the above adjacent strophes. Wagner, too, uses the two forms interchangeably, but distinguishes the full line typographically from the half-line:

O traut' er Mime	Oh, let him beware
dem treulosen, nicht!	of the treacherous dwarf!
Hörte Siegfried nur schärf	Oh, let Siegfried attend
auf des Schelmen Heuchlergered';	to the crafty words Mime speaks!
wie sein Herz es meint,	What he really means
kann er Mime versteh'n;	you will now understand,
so nützt' ihm des Blutes Genüss	made wise by the taste of the blood.

The foregoing example is a skilful literary pastiche, but far too often the result comes dangerously close to parody. Ettmüller himself advised against secondary alliteration of the weakly stressed syllables and the coinage of pseudo-archaic expressions (although, as the above passages reveal, he was himself occasionally guilty of these excesses): Wagner, however, had no such inhibitions. Indeed, the premises upon which his argument was built persuaded him that the more insistent the *Stabreim* and the more archaic the language, the more 'authentic' the text of *The Ring* would be as an expression of 'purely human' emotions. The resultant 'alliterative stuttering' has often been commented on, and whole dictionaries have been written to elucidate the text, a fact which English audiences are apt to ignore. The poetic diction of the Elder Edda is intensely compact and allusive, partly as a result of its strophic form (a feature which it shares with neither Anglo-Saxon nor Old High German poetry, where epic forms are preferred). By transferring an essentially lyric form to an epic drama and by mistaking the conscious and highly elaborate artistry of the Eddaic poems for a spontaneous outpouring of the popular spirit (an error he shared with the nineteenth century as a whole), Wagner has counterfeited a style which proves more of a hindrance than a help to our understanding of the text. It is significant that he largely abandoned *Stabreim* in his later librettos, and that in his open letter to Frédéric Villot in 1860, in which he summarised his aesthetic views of a decade earlier, he forbore to mention the device at all.

Wagner's craving for academic respectability (which for a time he thought he had found in the figure of Friedrich Nietzsche) is clear from his letter to the German philologist quoted above. It emerges even more clearly from his epitome of alleged sources for the libretto of *The Ring*, a list drawn up in January 1856 in response to an enquiry from Franz Müller. It runs as follows:

1. *Der Nibelunge Noth u. Klage* ed. by Lachmann.
2. *Zu den Nibelungen* etc. by Lachmann.
3. Grimm's *Mythology*.
4. *Edda*.
5. *Volsunga-Saga*, translated by Hagen-Breslau.
6. *Wilkina und Niflungasaga*, translated by Hagen-Breslau.
7. *Das deutsche Heldenbuch*, old edition, also updated by Hagen-Breslau. Revised edition in six volumes by Simrock.
8. *Die deutsche Heldensage* by Wilhelm Grimm.
9. *Untersuchungen zur deutschen Heldensage* by Mone.
10. *Heimskringla*, translated by Mohnike.

When King Ludwig II addressed a similar question to him in 1869, Wagner moderated his claims considerably, mentioning only the texts numbered 1, 4, 5, 8 and 9, and there is no doubt that he is here closer to the truth. This is not to say that Wagner did not read widely around the subject before committing his ideas to paper — the 200 volumes in his Dresden library and the 2,500 volumes in his later collection in Wahnfried attest to the breadth and depth of his reading throughout his life — but merely that the sources of *The Ring* are less extensive than has generally been supposed. It would have been possible for Wagner to have written *Die Nibelungensage (Mythus)* and *Die Wibelungen* on the basis of the *Nibelungenlied*, the two Eddas, the *Volsunga Saga* and Mone, although the task of reducing such disparate material to manageable form would have been facilitated by the critical writings of Ettmüller, Lachmann and von der Hagen.[3] It is tempting to speculate that the idea of writing an opera on the subject of Siegfried led Wagner to read the *Nibelungenlied*, which in turn brought him into contact with Lachmann's *Kritik der Sage von den Nibelungen* with its reconstructed myth of the fatal

3 There is strong evidence for believing in the additional influence of Heine's *Elementargeister* of 1837, Friedrich de la Motte Fouqué's *Sigurd der Schlangentödter* (Berlin 1808) and Carl Wilhelm Göttling's *Nibelungen und Gibelinen* (Rudolstadt 1816). The importance of the Grimms' 'Tale of the Youth who Left Home to Learn Fear' and Charles Perrault's *Le chat botté* has also long been recognised. I am less convinced by the alleged influence of *Les aventures merveilleuses du Prince Lyderic* by Alexandre Dumas *père* and of *Dr Fausts Hauskäppchen* by Friedrich Hopp (but see Newman's *Life* [1976 edition], II, 27-8 and 360-2).

Karl Christian Kohn as Fafner, Julia Varady as Freia and Franz Crass as Fasolt, Munich, 1975 (photo: Sabine Toepffer)

lure of gold. Wagner's interest in the other texts listed would then have followed as a matter of course.

When, in 1851, he resolved to expand *Siegfrieds Death* and turn the Grand Heroic Opera into a trilogy with a preceding evening, he had already left behind him his Dresden library, but the *Nibelungensage* scenario was sufficiently detailed in outline for him to be able to extrapolate from it the events of *The Young Siegfried, The Valkyrie* and, finally, *The Rhinegold*. And we know from Eliza Wille's reminiscences that Wagner's contact with Ettmüller during his years in Zurich was far greater than his autobiographical account would have us believe.

By the time he resumed work on *The Ring*, Wagner's attitude towards his material had changed: in 1848 Siegfried had been the mythical embodiment of necessary change, by 1851 he had become the symbolic incarnation of free will. The gods, whose theocracy had originally been ensured through Siegfried's vicarious atonement of their primeval guilt, were now foredoomed to perish in the world conflagration. *The Rhinegold* was written in part to tie up the loose ends at the beginning of the tetralogy, and in part to accommodate the new ideas on love and power which increasingly occupied Wagner's thoughts as a result of his reading of Feuerbach. In consequence of this, the sources of *The Rhinegold* are more disparate than for any of Wagner's earlier operas, inasmuch as there was no single narrative which could serve as its basis. Wagner was left to reconstruct and to invent more here than had been the case in the remaining parts of *The Ring* and, as Deryck Cooke has observed in *I Saw the World End*, 'We face the extraordinary fact that [the] opening scene of the tetralogy, despite its profoundly mythic character, is Wagner's own invention'. In the later scenes, too, we find Wagner 'adding features of his own' as well as 'taking over elements from the mythology, either unchanged, or compressed through certain omissions, or fused with one another, or altered in some way'. The great merit of Cooke's study was that it not only identified Wagner's borrowings; it was also alive to the intentional meaning of the tetralogy. As Cooke realised, it is not enough to list the primary and secondary sources of *The Ring*, unless we can also demonstrate why Wagner preferred certain versions to others and what his ultimate aim may have been in doing so. Nor is it sufficient to admire the joins and draw attention to the cracks in the surface structure of the work. For too long we have been distracted by the work's mythological fabric; only by stripping it away shall we penetrate the meaning of *The Ring* and cease to be daunted by what Gerhart Hauptmann called 'perhaps the most mystifying artistic creation of the last few thousand years'. A study of the sources of *The Ring* is a necessary first step in coming to an understanding of the cycle; it may teach us much about Wagner's work methods and help to throw light on the characters and their motivation. But *The Ring* will not give up its secrets until we are prepared to see it as a product of the mid-nineteenth century and as a Feuerbachian allegory of lust and love.

Thematic Guide

devised by

Lionel Friend

Each Opera Guide to a part of *The Ring* refers to one general list of leitmotifs in which the themes are numbered according to their first appearance in the cycle. For reference to later thematic guide numbers, readers are referred to the other titles in the series.

39

40

41

[21]

[22]

[23]

[24]   cf. [1b]

[25]

[26]

42

The Rhinegold
Das Rheingold

Preliminary Evening to the Festival Play
'The Ring of the Nibelung'

Music-Drama in Four Scenes
by Richard Wagner

Poem by Richard Wagner

English Translation by Andrew Porter

Das Rheingold was first performed in Munich on September 22, 1869. The first performance at the Festspielhaus, Bayreuth was on August 13, 1876. The first performance in England was at Her Majesty's Theatre, London in 1882. The first performance in America was in New York on January 4, 1889.

This translation was commissioned by English National Opera (then Sadler's Wells Opera) and first performed at the London Coliseum on March 1, 1972. The full cycle was first given in July and August 1973 and the opera was recorded in full performance at the London Coliseum in December 1975 by EMI.

The German text for the whole cycle was first published in 1853. Archaisms of spelling and an excess of punctuation have been removed but the original verse layout has been retained.

The stage directions are literal translations of those written by Wagner and do not reflect any actual production. The numbers in square brackets refer to the Thematic Guide.

CHARACTERS

Gods	Wotan	*bass-baritone*
	Donner	*baritone*
	Froh	*tenor*
	Loge	*tenor*
Giants	Fasolt	*bass-baritone*
	Fafner	*bass*
Nibelungs	Alberich	*bass-baritone*
	Mime	*tenor*
Goddesses	Fricka	*mezzo-soprano*
	Freia	*soprano*
	Erda	*contralto*
Rhinemaidens	Woglinde	*soprano*
	Wellgunde	*soprano*
	Flosshilde	*contralto*

Nibelungs

The Rhinemaidens mourn and the Nibelungs watch as the gods go up to Valhalla in Joachim Herz's Leipzig production, designed by Rudolf Heinrich (photo: Helga Vallmüller)

44

Scene One. *On the bed of the Rhine. Greenish twilight, brighter towards the top, darker below. The upper part of the stage is filled with swirling waters that flow restlessly from right to left. Towards the bottom, the waters resolve into an increasingly fine damp mist, so that a space a man's height from the ground seems to be completely free of the water, which courses like a train of clouds over the dusky bed. Craggy points of rock rise everywhere from the depths and mark the confines of the stage. The whole river bed is broken up into a craggy confusion, so that nowhere is it completely flat, and on all sides, in the dense darkness, there seem to be deeper gorges. The orchestra begins while the curtain is still closed.* [1a, 1b, 1c]

When the curtain rises, the watery depths are in full flood. In the centre of the stage, around a rock whose slender point reaches up into the brighter area of densely swirling water, one of the Rhinemaidens is circling with a graceful swimming motion.

WOGLINDE

Weia! Waga!	[2] Weia! Waga!
Wandering waters,	Woge, du Welle!
lulling our cradle!	Walle zur Wiege!
Wagalaweia!	Wagalaweia!
Wallala weiala weia!	Wallala weiala weia!

WELLGUNDE'S VOICE
(*from above*)

Woglinde, watching alone?	Woglinde, wachst du allein?

WOGLINDE

Till Wellgunde joins me below.	Mit Wellgunde wär' ich zu zwei.

WELLGUNDE
(*dives down from the waters to the rock.*)

Let's see how you watch!	Lass sehn, wie du wachst.

She tries to catch Woglinde.

WOGLINDE
(*swims away from her.*)

Safe from your grasp!	Sicher vor dir.

They tease and playfully try to catch one another. [1c]

FLOSSHILDE'S VOICE
(*from above*)

Heiala weia!	Heiala weia!
Careful, my sisters!	Wildes Geschwister!

WELLGUNDE

Flosshilde, swim!	Flosshilde, schwimm!
Woglinde flies:	Woglinde flieht:
hurry and help me to catch her!	hilf mir die Fliehende fangen!

FLOSSHILDE
(*dives down and comes between them in their play.*)

The sleeping gold	Des Goldes Schlaf
calls for your care!	hütet ihr schlecht;
Back to your task	besser bewacht
of guarding its bed,	des Schlummernden Bett,
or else you'll pay for your games!	sonst büsst ihr beide das Spiel!

With merry cries the other two separate; Flosshilde tries to catch first one, then the other; they elude her, and then join again in pursuit of her; thus they dart like fish from rock to rock, playing and laughing.
Meanwhile Alberich, clambering up a rock, has emerged from a dark chasm at the bottom. He pauses, still surrounded by darkness, and with increasing pleasure watches the water-maidens at play.

He, he! You nixies!
What a delightful,
delicate sight!
From Nibelheim's night
I would draw near
if I thought you'd be kind.

Hehe! Ihr Nicker!
Wie seid ihr niedlich,
neidliches Volk!
Aus Nibelheims Nacht
naht' ich mich gern
neigtet ihr euch zu mir.

At the sound of Alberich's voice, the maidens stop playing.

WOGLINDE

Hi, who is there?

Hei! wer ist dort?

FLOSSHILDE

A voice in the dark.

Es dämmert und ruft.

WELLGUNDE

Look who is below!

Lugt, wer uns belauscht!

They dive down deeper and see the Nibelung.

WOGLINDE AND WELLGUNDE

Pfui! He's horrible!

Pfui! der Garstige!

FLOSSHILDE
(*swiftly darting upwards*)

Be on your guard!
Father warned us
about such a foe.

Hütet das Gold!
Vater warnte
vor solchem Feind.

The others follow her, and all three swiftly gather round the central rock.

ALBERICH

You, above there!

Ihr, da oben!

ALL THREE

What want you, below there?

Was willst du dort unten?

ALBERICH

Only to stand
admiring your charming games;
then if you're friendly
you'll dive down
to the bottom, so I can join in!

Stör ich eu'r Spiel,
wenn staunend ich still hier steh?
Tauchtet ihr nieder,
mit euch tollte
und neckte der Niblung sich gern!

WOGLINDE

He wants us to join him?

Mit uns will er spielen?

WELLGUNDE

He must be mad!

Ist ihm das Spott?

ALBERICH

You shine and gleam
in the watery gloom!
How I would love
to enfold such maids in my arms:
please come join me below!

[5x] Wie scheint im Schimmer
ihr hell und schön!
Wie gern umschlänge
der Schlanken eine mein Arm,
schlüpfte hold sie herab!

FLOSSHILDE

I laugh at my fears;
the dwarf is in love!

Nun lach ich der Furcht:
der Feind ist verliebt.

WELLGUNDE

The languishing dwarf!

Der lüsterne Kauz!

46

Teach him a lesson!   Lasst ihn uns kennen!

She sinks to the top of the rock, the foot of which Alberich has reached.

ALBERICH

She sinks to the rock!   Die neigt sich herab.

WOGLINDE

Come closer to me!   Nun nahe dich mir!

ALBERICH
(*clambers with gnome-like agility towards the top of the rock, but keeps falling back.*)

Slimy, slippery,   Garstig glatter
slithery smoothness!   glitschriger Glimmer!
The slope's too steep!   Wie gleit ich aus!
My hands and my feet   Mit Händen und Füssen
cannot get any grip   nicht fasse noch halt ich
on the slippery surface!   das schlecke Geschlüpfer!
And the water   Feuchtes Nass
tickles my nostrils: füllt mir die Nase:
oh, curse this sneezing!   verfluchtes Niesen!

He has got close to Woglinde.

WOGLINDE
(*laughing*)

Sneezing tells me   Prustend naht
my lover is near!   meines Freiers Pracht!

ALBERICH

You're mine at last,   Mein Friedel sei,
you beautiful child!   du fräuliches Kind!

He tries to embrace her.

WOGLINDE
(*eluding him*)

If I am yours,   Willst du mich frein,
then follow me here!   so freie mich hier!

She dives to another rock.

ALBERICH
(*scratches his head.*)

Alas! you escape?   O weh; du entweichst?
Ah, come nearer!   Komm doch wieder!
You can swim,   Schwer ward mir,
but I stumble and slide.   was so leicht du erschwingst.

WOGLINDE
(*swims off to a third rock, further down.*)

Would you prefer   Steig nur zu Grund:
this rock at the bottom?   da greifst du mich sicher!

ALBERICH
(*clambers down hastily.*)

It's certainly safer!   Wohl besser da unten!

WOGLINDE
(*darts upwards to a high rock at the side.*)

And now to a high one!   Nun aber nach oben!

WELLGUNDE AND FLOSSHILDE

Hahahahaha!   Hahahahaha!

ALBERICH

Oh, how can I catch	Wie fang ich im Sprung
this flighty fish?	den spröden Fisch?
Wait for me, false one!	Warte, du Falshe!

He scrambles up after her.

WELLGUNDE
(has sunk to a deeper rock on the other side.)

Heia! fair lover,	Heia! Du Holder!
turn you this way.	Hörst du mich nicht?

ALBERICH
(turning towards her)

Calling to me?	Rufst du nach mir?

WELLGUNDE

And hear this advice:	Ich rate dir wohl:
Why chase Woglinde?	zu mir wende dich,
Wellgunde calls you!	Woglinde meide!

ALBERICH
(hastily clambering over the bottom towards Wellgunde.)

And you are fairer still	Viel schöner bist du
than your sister,	als jene Scheue,
who gleams less brightly,	die minder gleissend
who's far too sleek.	und gar zu glatt.
Now come towards me	Nur tiefer tauche,
so I can clasp you!	willst du mir taugen!

WELLGUNDE
(descending a shade closer towards him)

Well, now am I near?	Bin nun ich dir nah?

ALBERICH

Not near enough!	Noch nicht genug!
Those lovely arms	Die schlanken Arme
come twine round my neck,	schlinge um mich,
so I can touch you	dass ich den Nacken
and play with your tresses,	dir neckend betaste,
and fondle your breasts	mit schmeichelnder Brunst
in my passionate, burning embraces!	an die schwellende Brust mich dir
	schmiege!

WELLGUNDE

So you're in love	Bist du verliebt
and longing to hold me;	und lüstern nach Minne,
let's see, my beauty,	lass sehn, du Schöner,
just what you are like?	wie bist du zu schaun?
Pfui! You hairy old	Pfui, du haariger,
hideous imp!	höckriger Geck!
Scaly, spotted	Schwarzes, schwieliges
and sulphurous dwarf!	Schwefelgezwerg!
Look for a sweetheart	Such dir ein Friedel,
black as yourself!	dem du gefällst!

ALBERICH
(trying to hold her by force)

What though I am black —	Gefall ich dir nicht,
you're tight in my grasp!	dich fass ich doch fest!

WELLGUNDE
(swiftly diving away to the central rock)

So tight, I slip from your hands!	Nur fest, sonst fliess ich dir fort!

48

Hahahahaha!

Hahahahaha!

ALBERICH

Faithless thing!
Bony, cold-blooded fish!
So I'm not handsome,
pretty and playful,
slim and sleek —
Eh! Make love with an eel, then,
if he's more to your taste!

Falsches Kind!
Kalter, grätiger Fisch!
[5x] Schein ich nicht schön dir,
niedlich und neckisch,
glatt und glau —
hei! so buhle mit Aalen,
ist dir eklig mein Balg!

FLOSSHILDE

Stop grumbling, dwarf.
So soon dismayed?
With two you have failed!
Try now the third one.
Seek her love;
she may console your grief!

Was zankst du, Alp?
Schon so verzagt?
Du freitest um zwei!
Frügst du die dritte,
[4x] süssen Trost
schüfe die Traute dir!

ALBERICH

Lovely sounds
ravish my ears!
What luck to find
three of them here;
for one of the three may accept me
while one alone would reject me!
Show I can trust you,
and glide to my arms!

Holder Sang
singt zu mir her.
Wie gut, dass ihr
eine nicht seid!
Von vielen gefall ich wohl einer:
bei einer kieste mich keine!
Soll ich dir glauben,
so gleite herab!

FLOSSHILDE
(*dives down to Alberich.*)

O foolish sisters,
blind to beauty,
can't you see that he's fair?

Wie törig seid ihr,
dumme Schwestern,
dünkt euch dieser nicht schön!

ALBERICH
(*approaching her*)

And I declare them
stupid and ugly,
now that the loveliest is mine!

Für dumm und hässlich
darf ich sie halten,
seit ich dich Holdeste seh.

FLOSSHILDE
(*cajolingly*)

Oh, sing your song
so soft and sweet:
your voice bewitches my ear!

O singe fort
so süss und fein:
wie hehr verführt es mein Ohr!

ALBERICH
(*caressing her fondly*)

My heart bounds
and flutters and burns,
hearing this praise from your lips.

Mir zagt, zuckt
und zehrt sich das Herz,
lacht mir so zierliches Lob.

FLOSSHILDE
(*gently restraining him*)

Oh, how your beauty
delights my eyes,
and your smile so tender
inspires my soul!

Wie deine Anmut
mein Aug erfreut,
deines Lächelns Milde
den Mut mir labt!

She draws him tenderly towards her.

Dearest of men!

Seligster Mann!

ALBERICH

Sweetest of maids!

Süsseste Maid!

49

Now you are mine!	Wärst du mir hold!

Faithful for ever.	Hielt' ich dich immer!

(holding him close in her arms)

Oh, the sting of your glance,	Deinen stechenden Blick,
and the prick of your beard —	deinen struppigen Bart,
Oh, how they have captured my heart!	o säh' ich ihn, fasst' ich ihn stets!
And the locks of your hair,	Deines stachligen Haares
so shaggy and sharp,	strammes Gelock,
must float round Flosshilde ever!	umflöss' es Flosshilde ewig!
And your shape like a toad,	Deine Krötengestalt,
and the croak of your voice —	deiner Stimme Gekrächz,
Oh, how they ravish my soul:	o dürft ich staunend und stumm
I want nothing but these!	sie nur hören und sehn!

Hahahahahaha!	Hahahahahaha!

(starting from Flosshilde's embrace in alarm)

Are they daring to laugh?	Lacht ihr Bösen mich aus?

(suddenly darting away from him)

And laughter's the end of my song!	Wie billig am Ende vom Lied.

She dives quickly upward with her sisters.

Hahahahahaha!	Hahahahahaha!

(screeching)

Sorrow! oh sorrow!	[5x] Wehe! ach wehe!
Oh, shame! Oh, shame!	O Schmerz! O Schmerz!
The third one, so dear,	Die dritte, so traut,
betrays me as well.	betrog sie mich auch?
You shameless, slippery,	Ihr schmählich schlaues,
underhand, infamous wretches!	lüderlich schlechtes Gelichter!
Shifty and sly,	Nährt ihr nur Trug,
you treacherous watery tribe!	ihr treuloses Nickergezücht?

Wallala! Lalaleia! Leialalei!	[2] Wallala! Lalaleia! Leialalei!
Heia! Heia! Haha!	Heia! Heia! Haha!
Shame on you, Alberich!	Schäme dich, Albe!
Stop your complaining!	Schilt nicht dort unten!
Wait, and hear what we tell you!	Höre, was wir dich heissen!
You foolish Nibelung,	Warum, du Banger,
you should have held us	bandest du nicht
tightly while you could.	das Mädchen, das du minnst?
You'll find	Treu sind wir
that we can be true	und ohne Trug
and faithful, once we are caught!	dem Freier, der uns fängt.
Back to the chase	Greife nur zu
and grab without fear!	und grause dich nicht!
In the waves it's hard to escape.	In der Flut entfliehn wir nicht leicht.
Wallala! Lalaleia! Leialalei!	Wallala! Lalaleia! Leialala!
Heia! Heia! Hahei!	Heia! Heia! Hahei!

They swim apart, hither and thither, now deeper, now higher, inciting Alberich to pursue them.

Passionate fevers,
fervid desires,
have set me on fire!
Rage and longing,
wild and frantic,
drive me to madness!
Though you may laugh and lie,
yearning conquers my heart
and I'll not rest till I've caught you!

Wie in den Gliedern
brünstige Glut
mir brennt und glüht!
Wut und Minne
wild und mächtig
wühlt mir den Mut auf!
Wie ihr auch lacht und lügt,
lüstern lechz ich nach euch,
und eine muss mir erliegen!

He sets out in pursuit with desperate exertions; with terrible agility he clambers from rock to rock, leaps from one to another, tries to catch first one, then another of the maidens, who always elude him with merry cries. He stumbles, tumbles down to the bottom, then climbs quickly up to the heights again for a further chase. They lower themselves a little. He almost reaches them but again tumbles down, and tries once more. At last he stops, foaming with rage and breathless, and shakes his clenched fists up at the maidens.

ALBERICH
(*almost out of control*)

One, I swear, shall be mine...   Fing' eine diese Faust!...

He remains speechless with rage, looking upwards, and then is suddenly attracted and spellbound by the following spectacle. Through the waters an increasingly bright light makes its way from above, gradually kindling, on a high point of the central rock, to a dazzling, brightly-beaming gleam of gold; a magical golden light streams through the waters from this point. [3]

WOGLINDE

Look, sisters!
The sunlight is greeting the gold.

Lugt, Schwestern!
Die Weckerin lacht in den Grund.

WELLGUNDE

Through the watery gloom
she calls to the sleeper to wake.

Durch den grünen Schwall
den wonnigen Schläfer sie grüsst.

FLOSSHILDE

She kisses his eyelids,
tells them to open.

Jetzt küsst sie sein Auge,
dass er es öffne.

WELLGUNDE

See him smile now
with gentle light.

Schaut, es lächelt
in lichtem Schein.

WOGLINDE

Through the floods afar
shines his glittering beam.

Durch die Fluten hin
fleisst sein strahlender Stern.

ALL THREE
(*swimming together gracefully around the rock*)

Heiajaheia!   [4y]   Heiajaheia!
Heiajaheia!   Heiajaheia!
Wallalallalala leiajahei!   Wallalallalala leiajahei!
Rhinegold!   [4x]   Rheingold!
Rhinegold!   Rheingold!
Radiant joy!   Leuchtende Lust,
We laugh in your joyful shine!   wie lachst du so hell und hehr!
Glorious beams   Glühender Glanz
that glitter and gleam in the waves!   entgleisset dir weihlich im Wag!
Heiajahei!   Heiajahei!
Heiajaheia!   Heiajaheia!
Waken, friend!   Wache, Freund,
Wake in joy!   wache froh!
Wonderful games   Wonnige Spiele
we'll play in your praise: spenden wir dir:
flash in the foam,   flimmert der Fluss,

51

flame in the flood,	flammet die Flut,
and floating around you,	umfliessen wir tauchend,
dancing and singing,	tanzend und singend,
in joy we will dive to your bed!	im seligen Bade dein Bett.
Rhinegold!	Rheingold!
Rhinegold!	Rheingold!
Heiajaheia!	Heiajaheia!
Wallalaleia heiajahei!	Wallalaleia heiajahei!

With increasingly exuberant joy, the maidens swim round the rock. All the waters are a-glitter with the golden radiance. [3]

ALBERICH

(*whose eyes are powerfully attracted to the gleam, stares fixedly at the gold.*)

| What's that, you nymphs, | Was ist's, ihr Glatten, |
| up there, that shines and gleams? | das dort so glänzt und gleisst? |

THE THREE RHINEMAIDENS

| Ignorant dwarf, where have you lived? | Wo bist du Rauher denn heim, |
| Of the Rhinegold have you not heard? | dass vom Rheingold nie du gehört? |

WELLGUNDE

The dwarf's not heard	Nichts weiss der Alp
of the golden radiance	von des Goldes Auge,
which sleeps and wakes in turn?	das wechselnd wacht und schläft?

WOGLINDE

In the watery deeps	Von der Wassertiefe
this wonderful star	wonnigem Stern,
shines forth and brightens the waves.	der hehr die Wogen durchhellt?

ALL THREE

Ah, how gladly	Sieh, wie selig
we glide in its radiance!	im Glanze wir gleiten!
Come to join us	Willst du Banger
and bathe in brightness,	in ihm dich baden,
come sport and swim in the shine!	[2] so schwimm und schwelge mit uns!
Wallalalala leialalei!	[3] Wallalalala leialalei!
Wallalalala leiajahei!	Wallalalala leiajahei!

ALBERICH

Is that all it's good for,	Eurem Taucherspiele
to shine at your games?	nur taugte das Gold?
Why, then it is worthless!	Mir galt' es dann wenig!

WOGLINDE

This golden charm	Des Goldes Schmuck
you would revere,	schmähte er nicht,
oh, if you knew of its marvels!	wüsste er all seine Wunder!

WELLGUNDE

The world's wealth can	[6] Der Welt Erbe
be won by a man who,	gewänne zu eigen,
seizing the Rhinegold,	wer aus dem Rheingold
fashions a ring:	schüfe den Ring,
that ring makes him lord of the world.	der masslose Macht ihm verlieh'.

FLOSSHILDE

Our father told us,	Der Vater sagt' es,
but then he warned us	und uns befahl er,
we should guard it	klug zu hüten
and keep it safe,	den klaren Hort,
lest some false one should wickedly steal it:	dass kein Falscher der Flut ihn entführe:
be quiet, you chattering fools!	drum schweigt, ihr schwatzendes Heer!

52

	WELLGUNDE
My prudent sister,	Du klügste Schwester,
no need to be cross!	verklagst du uns wohl?
Surely you know	Weisst du denn nicht,
all that's required	wem nur allein
of him who would master the gold?	das Gold zu schmieden vergönnt?

	WOGLINDE
He must pronounce	[7a] Nur wer der Minne
a curse on love,	Macht versagt,
he must renounce	nur wer der Liebe
all joys of love,	Lust verjagt,
before he masters the magic,	nur der erzielt sich den Zauber,
a ring to forge from the gold.	[6] zum Reif zu zwingen das Gold.

	WELLGUNDE
And that's a thing	Wohl sicher sind wir
that will never be:	und sorgenfrei:
all men who live must love;	denn was nur lebt, will lieben;
no one could ever renounce it.	meiden will keiner die Minne.

	WOGLINDE
And least of all he,	Am wenigsten er,
that lecherous dwarf,	der lüsterne Alp:
all hot desire,	vor Liebesgier
panting with lust!	möcht er vergehn!

	FLOSSHILDE
Well, I confess	Nicht fürcht ich den,
we've nothing to fear.	wie ich ihn erfand:
I was nearly scorched	seiner Minne Brunst
when he came near.	brannte fast mich.

	WELLGUNDE
A sulphur-brand	Ein Schwefelbrand
in the swirling waves,	in der Wogen Schwall:
inflamed with longing,	vor Zorn der Liebe
sizzling loud!	zischt er laut.

	ALL THREE
Wallala! Wallaleialala!	[2] Wallala! Wallaleialala!
Loveliest Niblung,	Lieblichster Albe,
share in our joy.	lachst du nicht auch?
In the golden radiance,	In des Goldes Schein
how handsome you seem!	wie leuchtest du schön!
Oh come, lovely one, laugh and be glad!	O komm, Lieblicher, lache mit uns!
Heiajaheia! Heiajaheia!	Heiajaheia! Heiajaheia!
Wallalalala leiajahei!	[3] Wallalalala leiajahei!

They swim up and down in the glow, laughing.

ALBERICH
(his eyes fixed on the gold, has listened attentively to the sisters' chatter.) [6]

The world's wealth	Der Welt Erbe
can be mine if I utter the curse?	gewänn' ich zu eigen durch dich?
Though love be denied me,	Erzwäng ich nicht Liebe,
yet cunning can bring me delight?	[7a] doch listig erzwäng' ich mir Lust?
	(terribly loud)
Laugh if you will!	Spottet nur zu!
the Niblung's near to your toy!	Der Niblung naht eurem Spiel!

Furiously, he leaps across to the central rock and clambers up towards its summit in dreadful haste. The maidens separate with screams and swim upward in various directions.

53

Heia! Heia! Heiajahei!   Heia! Heia! Heiajahei!
Save yourselves!   Rettet euch!
The dwarf has gone mad;   Es raset der Alp!
and the water swirls   In den Wassern sprüht's,
where he has leapt.   wohin er springt:
His love has cost him his wits!   die Minne macht ihn verrückt!

They laugh with the wildest bravado

ALBERICH
(reaches the summit of the rock with one last bound.)

Still not afraid?   Bangt euch noch nicht?
Then laugh in the darkness,   So buhlt nun im Finstern,
nymphs of the waves!   feuchtes Gezücht!

He reaches out his hand towards the gold. [3]

Your light yields to my hand: Das Licht lösch ich euch aus;
I'll seize from the rock your gold,   entreisse dem Riff das Gold,
forge that magical ring.   schmiede den rächenden Ring;
Now hear me, you floods: [6]   denn hör es die Flut:
Love, I curse you for ever!   [7a]   so verfluch ich die Liebe!

With terrible force, he tears the gold from the rock [3] *and hastily plunges down with it into the depths, where he quickly disappears. Thick darkness suddenly descends on everything. The maidens rapidly dive down after the robber into the depths.*

FLOSSHILDE

Capture the robber!   Haltet den Räuber!

WELLGUNDE

Rescue the gold!   Rettet das Gold!

WOGLINDE AND WELLGUNDE

Help us! Help us!   Hilfe! Hilfe!

ALL THREE

Woe! Woe!   Weh! Weh!

The waters sink down with them into the depths. From the lowest depth, Alberich's harsh, mocking laughter is heard. The rocks disappear in the thick darkness; the whole stage is filled from top to bottom with black billowing water, which for some time seems to be continually sinking. [7a, 6]

Scene Two. *The waves are gradually transformed into clouds, which, as an increasingly brighter dawn light passes behind them, resolve into fine mist. When the mist has completely vanished aloft in gentle little clouds, in the dawning light an open space on a mountain height becomes visible. The daybreak illuminates with increasing brightness a castle with gleaming battlements, which stands on a rocky summit in the background. Between this and the foreground of the stage a deep valley is to be imagined, through which the Rhine flows. Wotan and, beside him, Fricka, both asleep, are lying on a flowery bank at one side. The castle has become completely visible.* [8]

FRICKA
(wakes; her eyes fall on the castle; she starts in alarm.)

Wotan, my lord! Awaken!   Wotan, Gemahl! Erwache!

WOTAN
(gently, still dreaming) [6]

The sacred hall of the gods   Der Wonne seligen Saal
is guarded by gate and door: bewachen mir Tür und Tor:
manhood's honour,   [8b]   Mannes Ehre,
unending power,   ewige Macht
rise now to endless renown!   ragen zu endlosem Ruhm!

FRICKA
(shakes him.)

Up from your dreams	Auf, aus der Träume
of flattering deceit!	wonnigem Trug!
My husband, wake and consider!	Erwache, Mann, und erwäge!

WOTAN

(wakes and raises himself a little; his eyes are at once attracted by the sight of the castle.) [8]

Completed, the eternal work!	Vollendet das ewige Werk:
On mountain summits	auf Berges Gipfel
the gods will rule!	die Götterburg
Proudly rise	prächtig prahlt
those glittering walls	der prangende Bau!
which in dreams I designed,	Wie im Traum ich ihn trug,
which my will brought to life.	wie mein Wille ihn wies,
Strong and lordly	stark und schön
see it shine;	steht er zur Schau;
holy, glorious abode!	hehrer, herrlicher Bau!

FRICKA

Though it delights you,	Nur Wonne schafft dir.
I am afraid!	was mich erschreckt?
You have your hall,	Dich freut die Burg,
but I think of Freia!	mir bangt es um Freia.
Can I believe you have forgotten	Achtloser, lass dich erinnern
the price you still have to pay?	des ausbedungenen Lohns!
The work is finished,	[9a] Die Burg ist fertig,
the giants must be paid;	verfallen das Pfand:
remember it, all that you owe!	[12] vergassest du, was du vergabst?

WOTAN

I've not forgotten the bargain,	Wohl dünkt mich's, was sie bedangen,
the giants shall have their reward;	die dort die Burg mir gebaut;
for that proud race	[9a] durch Vertrag zähmt' ich
was subdued by my spear;	ihr trotzig Gezücht,
graved on its shaft	dass sie die hehre
the terms for the castle.	Halle mir schüfen;
It stands now; thank the workers,	die steht nun — Dank den Starken:
and forget what it will cost.	um den Sold sorge dich nicht.

FRICKA

What carefree, frivolous lightness!	O lachend frevelnder Leichtsinn!
Loveless, coldhearted folly!	Liebelosester Frohmut!
If I had known of your deal,	Wusst' ich um euren Vertrag,
I might have stopped it in time;	dem Truge hätt' ich gewehrt;
but slyly you men	doch mutig entferntet
did your talking in secret,	ihr Männer die Frauen,
and kept us women away;	um taub und ruhig vor uns
alone you discussed with the giants.	allein mit den Riesen zu tagen.
Then to your shame	So ohne Scham
you promised to give them	verschenktet ihr Frechen
Freia, my beautiful sister;	Freia, mein holdes Geschwister,
oh, how pleased you were then!	froh des Schächergewerbs.
Nothing is sacred,	Was ist euch Harten
you harden your hearts,	doch heilig und wert,
when you men lust for might!	giert ihr Männer nach Macht!

WOTAN
(calmly) [6]

And is Fricka	Gleiche Gier
free from reproach?	war Fricka wohl fremd,
Remember, you begged for the hall!	also selbst um den Bau sie mich bat?

FRICKA

For I wished you faithful and true;
my thoughts were for my husband,
how to keep him beside me
when he was tempted to roam:
safe in our castle,
calm and contented, [10]
there I might keep you
in peaceful repose.
But you, when you planned it, [12]
thought of war and arms alone:
glory and might
all that you cared for;
you built it for storm and adventure —
constructed a fort, not a home.

Um des Gatten Treue besorgt,
muss traurig ich wohl sinnen,
wie an mich er zu fesseln,
zieht's in die Ferne ihn fort:
herrliche Wohnung,
wonniger Hausrat
sollten dich binden
zu säumender Rast.
Doch du bei dem Wohnbau sannst
auf Wehr und Wall allein:
Herrschaft und Macht
soll er dir mehren;
nur rastlosern Sturm zu erregen,
erstand dir die ragende Burg.

WOTAN
(*smiling*)

Wife, though you wish me [10]
confined in the castle,
some freedom still you must grant me;
though I may stay
beside you, yet
from our home I must rule all the world; [8b]
wandering and change
inspire my heart;
that sport I cannot relinquish!

Wolltest du Frau
in der Feste mich fangen,
mir Gotte musst du schon gönnen,
dass, in der Burg
gefangen, ich mir
von aussen gewinne die Welt.
Wandel und Wechsel
liebt, wer lebt:
das Spiel drum kann ich nicht sparen.

FRICKA

Cruel, heartless,
unloving man!
For the vain delights of
ruling the world,
you'd carelessly gamble away
love and woman's worth?

Liebeloser,
leidigster Mann!
Um der Macht und Herrschaft
müssigen Tand
verspielst du in lästerndem Spott
[7a] Liebe und Weibes Wert?

WOTAN
(*serious*)

Recall the days when I wooed you, [9a]
when I for Fricka
paid the price of an eye.
Your scolding is wide of the mark!
I worship women
much more than you'd like;
and Freia, the fair one,
I shall not yield;
such thoughts were far from my mind.

Um dich zum Weib zu gewinnen,
mein eines Auge
setzt' ich werbend daran:
wie törig tadelst du jetzt!
Ehr ich die Frauen
doch mehr, als dich freut!
Und Freia, die gute,
geb ich nicht auf:
nie sann dies ernstlich mein Sinn.

FRICKA
(*with anxious tension, looking off-stage*)

Then shelter her now;
defenceless, afraid,
see how she runs here for help!

So schirme sie jetzt;
in schutzloser Angst
läuft sie nach Hilfe dort her!

FREIA
(*enters hurriedly, in flight.*) [11]

Help me, sister!
Shelter me, brother!
On yonder mountain
Fasolt is threatening,
and now he's coming to take me.

Hilf mir, Schwester!
Schütze mich, Schwäher!
Vom Felsen drüben
drohte mir Fasolt,
[12] mich Holde käm' er zu holen.

WOTAN

Let him come!
Saw you not Loge?

Lass ihn drohn!
Sahst du nicht Loge?

56

In that infamous rogue
do you still put your trust?
Much harm he's done to the gods,
yet time and again you still use him.

Dass am liebsten du immer
dem Listigen traust!
Viel Schlimmes schuf er uns schon,
doch stets bestrickt er dich wieder.

WOTAN

Where simple truth serves,
I need no one to help me;
but to use the hate
of foes to serve me —
that needs guile and deceit;
then Loge's the one for the deed.
He said he'd think of a plan
to keep our Freia in safety;
so I rely on him now.

Wo freier Mut frommt,
allein frag ich nach keinem;
doch des Feindes Neid
zum Nutz sich fügen,
lehrt nur Schlauheit und List,
wie Loge verschlagen sie übt.
Der zum Vertrage mir riet,
versprach mir Freia zu lösen:
auf ihn verlass ich mich nun.

FRICKA

And he leaves you alone!
Here come the giants   [12]
seeking their pay,
while Loge loiters afar!

Und er lässt dich allein!
Dort schreiten rasch
die Riesen heran:
wo harrt dein schlauer Gehilf?

FREIA

Come here to me, my brothers,   [11]
oh, help me and save me,
now that Wotan abandons the weak!

Wo harren meine Brüder,
dass Hilfe sie brächten,
da mein Schwäher die Schwache
verschenkt?
Oh, help me, Donner!   Zu Hilfe, Donner!
Hear me, help me!   Hieher, hieher!
Rescue Freia, my Froh!   Rette Freia, mein Froh!

FRICKA

The disgraceful men who betrayed you
have all abandoned you now!

Die im bösen Bund dich verrieten,
sie alle bergen sich nun.

Fasolt and Fafner enter, both of gigantic stature, and armed with stout clubs. [12]

FASOLT

Soft sleep
closed your eyes,
while we were working
hard to build your hall.
Working hard,
day and night,
heavy stones
we heaped up high,
lofty towers,
gates and doors,
guard and keep
your castle walls secure.

Sanft schloss
Schlaf dein Aug:
wir beide bauten
Schlummers bar die Burg.
Mächt'ger Müh
müde nie,
stauten starke
Stein' wir auf;
steiler Turm,
Tür und Tor
deckt und schliesst
im schlanken Schloss den Saal.
(pointing to the castle) [8b]

There stands
what you ordered,
shining bright
in morning light.
There's your home;
we want our wage!

Dort steht's,
was wir stemmten;
schimmernd hell
bescheint's der Tag:
zieh nun ein,
[12] uns zahl den Lohn!

WOTAN

You've earned your reward;
what wages are you asking?

Nennt, Leute, den Lohn:
was dünkt euch zu bedingen?

FASOLT

The price was fixed,   [9a]
our bargain was made;

Bedungen ist's,
was tauglich uns dünkt:

57

have you so soon forgot?	gemahnt es dich so matt?
Freia, the fair one,	[11] Freia, die holde,
Holda, the free one —	Holda, die freie —
your hall is built	vertragen ist's —
and Freia is ours.	sie tragen wir heim.

WOTAN
(*quickly*)

Plainly your work	Seid ihr bei Trost
has blinded your wits.	mit eurem Vertrag?
Ask some other wage:	Denkt auf andren Dank:
Freia cannot be sold.	Freia ist mir nicht feil.

FASOLT
(*utterly amazed, is for a moment speechless.*) [9a]

What's this now? Ha!	Was sagst du? Ha,
Breaking your bond?	sinnst du Verrat?
Betraying your word?	Verrat am Vertrag?
On your spear shaft,	[9a] Die dein Speer birgt,
read what is graved;	sind sie dir Spiel,
would you dare to break your bargain?	des beratnen Bundes Runen?

FAFNER
(*scornfully*)

My trusting brother,	Getreuster Bruder!
now do you see his deceit?	Merkst du Tropf nun Betrug?

FASOLT

God of light,	Lichtsohn du,
light of spirit!	leicht gefügter,
Hear a giant's advice,	hör und hüte dich:
and learn to keep your word!	Verträgen halte Treu!
What you are,	Was du bist,
you became by your bargains;	bist du nur durch Verträge:
you base your power	bedungen ist,
on the bonds there defined.	wohl bedacht deine Macht.
Since you are wise,	Bist weiser du,
we giants were bound;	als witzig wir sind,
freely we promised	bandest uns Freie
to keep the peace;	zum Frieden du:
yet I shall curse your wisdom;	all deinem Wissen fluch ich,
war, not peace, will reward you	fliehe weit deinen Frieden,
if you don't fairly,	[15] weisst du nicht offen,
frankly uphold	ehrlich und frei
the terms of the bargain you swore!	Verträgen zu wahren die Treu!
This simple giant	Ein dummer Riese
speaks his mind:	rät dir das:
you wise one, learn now from him.	du, Weiser, wiss' es von ihm!

WOTAN

How sly to take in earnest	Wie schlau für Ernst du achtest,
what as a joke we decided!	was wir zum Scherz nur beschlossen!
The beautiful goddess,	Die liebliche Göttin,
fair and bright,	licht und leicht,
what use can she be to you?	was taugt euch Tölpeln ihr Reiz?

FASOLT

How unjust!	Höhnst du uns?
Wotan mocks us!	Ha, wie unrecht!
You who through beauty reign,	[11a] Die ihr durch Schönheit herrscht,
glittering, glorious race,	schimmernd hehres Geschlecht,
like fools you yearned	[12] wie törig strebt ihr,
for your towers of stone;	nach Türmen von Stein,
pledged as pay for your hall	setzt um Burg und Saal
woman's beauty and grace.	[7a] Weibes Wonne zum Pfand!

58

We dull ones toil away,
sweat with our work-hardened hands;
we longed for a woman,
so charming and fair,
to grace our poor dwelling —
and you say all was a joke?

[12] Wir Plumpen plagen uns
schwitzend mit schwieliger Hand,
[11] ein Weib zu gewinnen,
das wonnig und mild
bei uns Armen wohne:
und verkehrt nennst du den Kauf?

FAFNER

Stop your foolish chatter;
the girl's not what we want.
Freia's charms
mean nothing,
but we gain
as soon as the gods have lost her.
Golden apples
ripen within her garden,
she alone
knows how they are tended;
that golden fruit
given to her kinsmen
each day renews
youth everlasting:
pale and grey
they'll lose all their beauty,
wan and weak
they will grow old,
when that fruit is denied them.
And that's why we'll take her away!

Schweig dein faules Schwatzen,
Gewinn werben wir nicht:
Freias Haft
hilft wenig;
doch viel gilt's,
den Göttern sie zu entführen.
[16a] Goldne Äpfel
wachsen in ihrem Garten;
sie allein
weiss die Äpfel zu pflegen!
Der Frucht Genuss
frommt ihren Sippen
zu ewig nie
alternder Jugend;
[16b] siech und bleich
doch sinkt ihre Blüte,
alt und schwach
schwinden sie hin,
müssen Freia sie missen.
Ihrer Mitte drum sei sie entführt!
[16a, 12]

WOTAN
(*aside*)

Loge lingers long!

Loge säumt zu lang!

FASOLT

Well, what shall it be?

Schlicht gib nun Bescheid!

WOTAN

Ask some other wage!

Sinnt auf andern Sold!

FASOLT

No other: Freia alone!

Kein andrer: Freia allein!

FAFNER

You there! Come with us!

Du da, folge uns!

They make towards Freia. Donner and Froh rush in.

FREIA
(*fleeing*)

Help! Help from these hard ones!

Helft, helft vor den Harten!

FROH
(*clasping Freia in his arms*) [16a]

To me, Freia!
Back from her, giant!
Froh shields the fair one!

Zu mir, Freia!
Meide sie, Frecher!
Froh schützt die Schöne.

DONNER
(*planting himself before the two giants*)

Fasolt and Fafner,
know you the weight
of my hammer's heavy blow?

Fasolt und Fafner,
fühltet ihr schon
meines Hammers harten Schlag?

FAFNER

What is this threat?

Was soll das Drohn?

59

What brings you here?	Was dringst du her?
We've not come to fight,	[12] Kampf kiesten wir nicht,
but all we want is our pay.	verlangen nur unsern Lohn.

DONNER

And I know	Schon oft zahlt' ich
how giants should be paid.	Riesen den Zoll;
Come here, receive your wage,	kommt her! Des Lohnes Last
weighed with a generous hand.	wäg ich mit gutem Gewicht!

He swings his hammer.

WOTAN
(*stretching out his spear between the disputants*) [9a]

Back, you wild one!	Halt, du Wilder!
Force will not serve!	Nichts durch Gewalt!
This bond is graved	Verträge schützt
on my spear's strong shaft:	meines Speeres Schaft:
spare them your hammer's blow!	spar deines Hammers Heft!

FREIA

Help me! Help me!	[11a, 5x] Wehe! Wehe!
Wotan forsakes me!	Wotan verlässt mich!

FRICKA

Is this your resolve,	Begreif ich dich noch,
merciless man?	grausamer Mann?

WOTAN
(*turns round and sees Loge approaching.*) [13a]

There is Loge!	[13b] Endlich Loge!
Where have you been,	[14] Eiltest du so,
you who assured me	den du geschlossen,
that I'd escape from this contract?	den schlimmen Handel zu schlichten?

LOGE
(*has climbed up from the valley at the back.*) [13a]

What? How am I	Wie? Welchen Handel
concerned in a contract?	[13b] härt ich geschlossen?
Do you mean that agreement	[14] Wohl was mit den Riesen
you have made with these giants?	[8] dort im Rate du dangst?
I roam through the whole wide	[13a] In Tiefen und Höhen
world as I please:	[8] treibt mich mein Hang;
I'm not held	[13a] Haus und Herd
by house or home.	behagt mir nicht:
Donner and Froh	Donner und Froh,
are dreaming of household joys!	die denken an Dach und Fach!
If they would wed,	Wollen sie frein,
a house first they must own.	ein Haus muss sie erfreun.
And castle walls,	Ein stolzer Saal,
and lofty halls,	ein starkes Schloss,
they were what Wotan craved.	danach stand Wotans Wunsch.
Lofty halls,	[8] Haus und Hof,
castle walls,	Saal und Schloss,
a home for the gods —	die selige Burg,
it stands there, strongly built.	sie steht nun fest gebaut;
I inspected all	das Prachtgemäuer
the place myself;	prüf' ich selbst;
it's firmly made,	ob alles fest,
safe and secure:	forscht' ich genau:
Fasolt and Fafner,	Fasolt und Fafner
excellent work!	fand ich bewährt;
No stone stirs on its bed.	kein Stein wankt im Gestemm.

So I was not lazy,
like others here;
he lies, who says that I was!

[13a] Nicht müssig war ich,
wie mancher hier:
der lügt, wer lässig mich schilt!

WOTAN

Don't try
to escape from the point!
If you betray me,
if you have tricked me, beware!
Recall that I
am your only friend,
I took your part
when the other gods were unkind.
So speak, I need your help!
When first those giants made terms
and asked Freia as payment,
you know I only
gave my consent
because you promised you would find
something else they would rather have.

Arglistig
weichst du mir aus:
mich zu betrügen
hüte in Treuen dich wohl!
Von allen Göttern
dein einz'ger Freund,
nahm ich dich auf
in der übel trauenden Tross.
Nun red und rate klug!
[9a] Da einst die Bauer der Burg
[13a] zum Dank Freia bedangen,
du weisst, nicht anders
willigt' ich ein,
als weil auf Pflicht du gelobtest,
zu lösen das hehre Pfand.

LOGE

I merely promised
I'd consider
how we might save her —
and that's all I said.
But to discover
what can't be found,
what never was —
who'd ever make such a promise?

Mit höchster Sorge
drauf zu sinnen,
wie es zu lösen,
[13b] das — hab ich gelobt.
[14] Doch dass ich fände,
was nie sich fügt,
was nie gelingt,
wie liess' sich das wohl geloben?

FRICKA
(to Wotan)

That's the knave
whom you thought you could trust!

Sieh, welch trugvollem
Schelm du getraut!

FROH

Loge, hear me,
your name should be Liar!

Loge heisst du,
doch nenn ich dich Lüge!

DONNER

Accursed Loge,
I'll quench your flame!

Verfluchte Lohe,
dich lösch ich aus!

LOGE

To conceal his blunders
every fool blames me!

Ihre Schmach zu decken
schmähen mich Dumme.

Donner threatens Loge.

WOTAN
(intervening)

Now cease reviling my friend!
You know not Loge's ways:
his advice
is worth all the more,
when we wait on his words.

In Frieden lasst mir den Freund!
Nicht kennt ihr Loges Kunst:
[19] reicher wiegt
seines Rates Wert,
zahlt er zögernd ihn aus.

FAFNER

Wait no longer!
Pay our wage!

[12] Nicht gezögert!
Rasch gezahlt!

FASOLT

Come, no more delay!

Lang währt's mit dem Lohn.

61

WOTAN

(turning sharply to Loge, urgently) [13a]

Speak out, stubborn one!	Jetzt hör, Störrischer!
Keep your word!	Halte Stich!
And tell me now where you've been.	Wo schweiftest du hin und her?

LOGE

Never one word	Immer ist Undank
of praise or thanks!	Loges Lohn!
For your sake alone,	Um dich nur besorgt,
hoping to help,	sah ich mich um,
I restlessly roamed	durchstöbert' im Sturm
to the ends of the earth,	alle Winkel der Welt,
to find a ransom for Freia,	Ersatz für Freia zu suchen,
one that the giants would like more.	wie er den Riesen wohl recht.
I sought vainly,	Umsonst sucht' ich
but one thing I learnt:	und sehe nun wohl,
in this whole wide world	in der Welten Ring
nothing at all	nichts ist so reich,
is of greater worth to a man	als Ersatz zu muten dem Mann
than woman's beauty and love!	[7b] für Weibes Wonne und Wert!

(All express astonishment and diverse forms of bewilderment.) [11a]

I asked every one living,	So weit Leben und Weben,
in water, earth, and sky,	in Wasser, Erd und Luft,
one question;	viel frug ich,
sought for the answer	forschte bei allen,
from all whom I met;	wo Kraft nur sich rührt
I asked them this question:	und Keime sich regen:
What in this world	was wohl dem Manne
means more to you	mächtiger dünk'
than woman's beauty and love?	als Weibes Wonne und Wert?
But wherever life was stirring	Doch so weit Leben und Weben,
they laughed at me	verlacht nur ward
when they heard what I asked.	meine fragende List:
In water, earth, and sky,	in Wasser, Erd und Luft
none would forego	lassen will nichts
the joys of love.	von Lieb und Weib.
But one I found then	Nur einen sah ich,
who scorned the delights of love,	der sagte der Liebe ab:
who valued gold	um rotes Gold
more dearly than woman's grace.	entriet er des Weibes Gunst.
The fair and shining Rhinemaids	[4] Des Rheines klare Kinder
came to me with their tale:	klagten mir ihre Not:
the Nibelung dwarf,	der Nibelung,
Alberich,	Nacht-Alberich,
begged for their favours,	[1c, 2] buhlte vergebens
but he begged them in vain;	um der Badenden Gunst;
the Rhinegold	das Rheingold da
he tore in revenge from their rock;	[3] raubte sich rächend der Dieb:
and now he holds it	[6] das dünkt ihm nun
dearer than love,	das teuerste Gut,
greater than woman's grace.	[7b] hehrer als Weibes Huld.
For their glittering toy,	[4] Um den gleissenden Tand,
thus torn from the deep,	der Tiefe entwandt,
the maidens are sadly mourning:	erklang mir der Töchter Klage:
they turn, Wotan,	an dich, Wotan,
sadly to you,	wenden sie sich,
for they hope that you will avenge them;	dass zu Recht du zögest den Räuber,
the gold — they pray	[3] das Gold dem Wasser
that you'll restore it,	wiedergebest,
to shine in the waters for ever.	[4] und ewig es bliebe ihr Eigen.
So I promised	Dir's zu melden
I'd tell you the story;	gelobt' ich den Mädchen:
and that's what Loge has done.	[13a] nun löste Loge sein Wort.

Are you mad,	Töng bist du,
or simply malicious?	wenn nicht gar tückisch!
You know I am in need;	Mich selbst siehst du in Not:
how can I help some one else?	wie hülf ich andern zum Heil?

FASOLT
(*who has been listening attentively, to Fafner*)

That gold I begrudge to Alberich;	Nicht gönn ich das Gold dem Alben,
we've suffered much from the Niblung,	viel Not schon schuf uns der Niblung,
and yet that crafty dwarf	doch schlau entschlüpfte
has always slipped through our hands.	unserm Zwange immer der Zwerg.

FAFNER

We shall suffer	Neue Neidtat
more in the future,	sinnt uns der Niblung,
now he's gained the gold.	gibt das Gold ihm Macht.
You there, Loge!	Du da, Loge!
Tell me the truth;	Sag ohne Lug:
what glory lies in the gold,	was Grosses gilt denn das Gold,
that the Niblung holds so dear?	dass es dem Niblung genügt?

LOGE

A toy, while	[4]	Ein Tand ist's
it was in the waters,		in des Wassers Tiefe,
lighting the Rhinemaidens' games;		lachenden Kindern zur Lust:
but when as a shining	[6]	doch, ward es zum runden
ring it is fashioned,		Reife geschmiedet,
helped by its magic power,		hilft es zur höchsten Macht,
its owner conquers the world.		gewinnt dem Manne die Welt.

WOTAN
(*reflectively*)

I have heard men tell	Von des Rheines Gold
of the Rhinegold:	hört' ich raunen:
charms of riches	Beute-Runen
lurk in that golden gleam;	berge sein roter Glanz,
mighty powers	Macht und Schätze
are his who can forge that ring.	schüf' ohne Mass ein Reif.

FRICKA
(*softly to Loge*)

Could a woman use	Taugte wohl
the golden ring	. des goldnen Tandes
for herself,	gleissend Geschmeid
and wear it to charm her lord?	auch Frauen zu schönem Schmuck?

LOGE

No husband dare		Des Gatten Treu
be false to his wife		ertrotzte die Frau,
when she commands	[10]	trüge sie hold
that glittering wealth		den hellen Schmuck,
that busy dwarves are forging,	[17]	den schimmernd Zwerge schmieden,
ruled by the power of the ring.		rührig im Zwange des Reifs.

FRICKA
(*cajolingly, to Wotan*) [11a]

Oh, how can my husband	Gewänne mein Gatte
win us the gold?	sich wohl das Gold?

WOTAN
(*seeming increasingly enchanted by his thoughts*) [3]

And I should possess it!	[6]	Des Reifes zu walten,
Soon this ring should be Wotan's.		rätlich will es mich dünken.

But say, Loge,
what is the art
by which the gold can be forged?

LOGE

A magic spell
can change the gold to a ring.
No one knows it,
but he who would use the spell
must curse the joys of love.

Wotan turns away angrily.

Could you do that?
Too late, in any case:
Alberich did not delay;
he cursed and mastered
the magic spell;
and he is lord of the ring!

DONNER
(*to Wotan*)

We shall all
be slaves to the dwarf
unless the ring can be captured.

WOTAN

The ring — I must have it!

FROH

Easily done,
now that love you need not renounce.

LOGE

Child's play!
At a stroke you can make it yours!

WOTAN
(*harshly*)

Then tell me, how?

LOGE

By theft!
What a thief stole,
you steal from the thief;
you seize it and make it your own!
But you'll need your wits
fighting Alberich;
he'll defend
what he has stolen,
so be skilful, swift, and shrewd
if you'd please the Rhinemaids,
and then restore
their gold, back to the waters.
They yearn and cry for their gold.

WOTAN

To please the Rhinemaids?
That's not what I plan!

FRICKA

Leave that watery brood
weeping and wailing;
to my distress,
many a man
they've lured by their charms to the Rhine.

Doch wie, Loge,
lernt' ich die Kunst?
Wie schüf' ich mir das Geschmeid?

LOGE

Ein Runenzauber
zwingt das Gold zum Reif.
Keiner kennt ihn;
[7a] doch einer übt ihn leicht,
der sel'ger Lieb entsagt.

Das sparst du wohl;
zu spät auch kämst du:
Alberich zauderte nicht;
[6] zaglos gewann er
des Zaubers Macht:
[7b] geraten ist ihm der Ring.

Zwang uns allen
schüfe der Zwerg,
würd' ihm der Reif nicht entrissen.

Den Ring muss ich haben!

Leicht erringt
ohne Liebesfluch er sich jetzt.

Spottleicht,
ohne Kunst wie im Kinderspiel!

So rate, wie?

Durch Raub!
Was ein Dieb stahl,
das stiehlst du dem Dieb:
[13a] ward leichter ein Eigen erlangt?
Doch mit arger Wehr
[3] wahrt sich Alberich;
[6] klug und fein
musst du verfahren,
ziehst du den Räuber zu Recht,
[4b] um des Rheines Töchtern
den roten Tand,
das Gold, wiederzugeben;
[3] denn darum flehen sie dich.

[4x] Des Rheines Töchter?
Was taugt mir der Rat?

Von dem Wassergezücht
mag ich nichts wissen:
schon manchen Mann
— mir zum Leid —
verlockten sie buhlend im Bad.

64

Philip Joll as Wotan and Nigel Douglas as Loge with (behind) Roderick Earle as Fafner, Welsh National Opera (photo: Zoë Dominic)

Wotan is struggling silently with himself. The other gods, tense and silent, look fixedly at him.
Meanwhile, to one side, Fafner has quietly been conferring with Fasolt.

FAFNER
(to Fasolt)

Trust me, more than Freia	[11a]Glaub mir, mehr als Freia
we can gain from the gold:	frommt das gleissende Gold:
eternal youth can be ours,	auch ew'ge Jugend erjagt,
when we lay our hands on that gold.	wer durch Goldes Zauber sie zwingt.

Fasolt's demeanour suggests that he has been persuaded against his will. [16a, 3] *Fafner, with Fasolt, returns to Wotan again.* [12]

Hear, Wotan,	Hör, Wotan,
I'll speak my last word!	der Harrenden Wort!
We will leave you with Freia;	Freia bleib' euch in Frieden;
we will take less	leichtren Lohn
for our payment:	fand ich zur Lösung:
for us rude giants, enough	uns rauhen Riesen genügt
is Nibelheim's shining gold.	des Niblungen rotes Gold.

WOTAN

Have you gone mad?	Seid ihr bei Sinn?
For how can I give you	Was nicht ich besitze,
what is not mine, as your payment?	soll ich euch Schamlosen schenken?

FAFNER

Hard labour	Schwer baute
built you those walls;	dort sich die Burg:
your cunning	leicht wird's dir
can lightly achieve	mit list'ger Gewalt,
what has proved too hard for our strength,	was im Neidspiel nie uns gelang,
to capture the Niblung foe.	[13a]den Niblungen fest zu fahn.

WOTAN

For you must I	Für euch müht' ich
deal with the Niblung?	mich um den Alben?
For you, capture the foe?	Für euch fing ich den Feind?
Unashamed, you dare	Unverschämt
to propose it,	und überbegehrlich
stupid, insolent pair!	macht euch Dumme mein Dank!

FASOLT
(suddenly seizes Freia and, with Fafner, pulls her to one side.)

Come here, maid!	Hieher, Maid!
You're in our power!	In unsre Macht!
We'll hold you as a hostage	Als Pfand folgst du uns jetzt,
till all has been paid!	bis wir Lösung empfahn.

FREIA
(crying out in dismay)

Save me! Save me! Woe!	Wehe! Wehe! Weh!

All the gods are dismayed.

FAFNER

We shall take	Fort von hier
Freia with us!	sei sie entführt!
Till evening, mark me well,	Bis Abend, achtet's wohl,
she remains in our hands;	pflegen wir sie als Pfand;
then we'll return;	wir kehren wieder;
but when we come,	doch kommen wir,
if we don't find what we have asked for,	und bereit liegt nicht als Lösung
the Rhinegold heaped on high —	[6] das Rheingold licht und rot —

— our truce then is over;
Freia is forfeit;
forever she stays with us!

Zu End ist die Frist dann,
Freia verfallen:
für immer folge sie uns!

FREIA
(*screaming*)

Sister! Brothers!
Save me! Help!

Schwester! Brüder!
Rettet! Helft!

She is dragged away by the giants as they hurry off.

FROH

On, to her aid!

Auf, ihnen nach!

DONNER

Everything's ended!

Breche denn alles!

They look inquiringly at Wotan.

FREIA
(*from the distance*)

Save me! Help!

[11a] Rettet! Helft!

LOGE
(*gazing after the giants*)

Over rock and stone they stride,
down to the vale;
through the Rhine they forge ahead,
waddling and wading.
Sad at heart
hangs Freia,
while borne on the backs of those ruffians!
Heia! hei!
They stumble and stride on their way!
Now they're through, climbing the slope.
They'll not rest till they've reached
rough Riesenheim's bounds.

Über Stock und Stein zu Tal
stapfen sie hin;
durch des Rheines Wasserfurt
waten die Riesen:
fröhlich nicht
hängt Freia
den Rauhen über dem Rücken!
Heia! hei!
Wie taumeln die Tölpel dahin!
Durch das Tal talpen sie schon:
wohl an Riesenheims Mark
erst halten sie Rast!

He turns to the gods.

Why is Wotan brooding and sad?
Alas, what's troubling the gods?

Was sinnt nun Wotan so wild?
[11a] Den seligen Göttern wie geht's?

A pale mist, growing denser, fills the scene; it gives the gods an increasingly wan and aged appearance: fearful, they all stand gazing expectantly at Wotan, who is lost in thought, his eyes fixed on the ground.

Mists, do you deceive me?
Is this a dream?
How grey you've grown,
so weary and weak!
From your cheeks the bloom dies out;
the flash from your eyes fades away!
Come, my Froh!
Day is still young!
From your hand, Donner,
you're dropping the hammer!
What's wrong with Fricka?
Can she be mourning
that Wotan, gloomy and grey,
should seem so suddenly old?

[11] Trügt mich ein Nebel?
[16a] Neckt mich ein Traum?
Wie bang und bleich
verblüht ihr so bald!
Euch erlischt der Wangen Licht;
der Blick eures Auges verblitzt!
Frisch, mein Froh,
noch ist's ja früh!
Deiner Hand, Donner,
entsinkt ja der Hammer!
Was ist's mit Fricka?
Freut sie sich wenig
[16b] ob Wotans grämlichem Grau,
das schier zum Greisen ihn schafft?

FRICKA

Sorrow! Sorrow!
What can it mean?

[5x] Wehe! Wehe!
Was ist geschehn?

DONNER

My hand is weak!

Mir sinkt die Hand.

67

My heart is still!

FROH

Mir stockt das Herz.

LOGE

I see now! Hear what is wrong!	Jetzt fand ich's: hört, was euch fehlt!
Of Freia's fruit	Von Freias Frucht
you've not yet eaten today.	genosset ihr heute noch nicht:
The golden apples	[16a] die goldnen Äpfel
that grow in her garden,	in ihrem Garten,
they kept you so vigorous and young,	sie machten euch tüchtig und jung,
eating them every day.	asst ihr sie jeden Tag.
But she who tended them	[16b] Des Gartens Pflegerin
now is a hostage;	ist nun verpfändet;
on the branches droops	an den Ästen darbt
and dies the fruit;	und dorrt das Obst:
it rots, falls to the ground.	[13a]bald fällt faul es herab.
To me it's nothing;	Mich kümmert's minder;
because to Loge	an mir ja kargte
Freia was mean;	Freia von je
I never tasted her fruit:	knausernd die köstliche Frucht:
so I'm not god-like,	denn halb so echt nur
I'm not so glorious as you!	[13b]bin ich wie, Selige, ihr!
But you staked your future	Doch ihr setztet alles
on that youth-giving fruit;	auf das jüngende Obst:
the giants knew that all too well;	das wussten die Riesen wohl;
and at your lives	auf euer Leben
this blow has been aimed;	legten sie's an:
so think how to escape!	nun sorgt, wie ihr das wahrt!
Lacking the apples,	[16a] Ohne die Äpfel,
old and grey,	alt und grau,
worn and weary,	greis und grämlich,
withered and scorned by the world,	welkend zum Spott aller Welt,
the gods grow old and die.	erstirbt der Götter Stamm.

FRICKA

Wotan, my lord!	Wotan, Gemahl,
Unhappy man!	unsel'ger Mann!
See how your selfish	Sieh, wie dein Leichtsinn
folly has brought us	lachend uns allen
sore disgrace and shame!	Schimpf und Schmach erschuf!

WOTAN
(*starts up with sudden resolve.*)

Come, Loge,	Auf, Loge,
descend with me!	hinab mit mir!
To Nibelheim we'll go together:	Nach Nibelheim fahren wir nieder:
and there I'll win me the gold.	gewinnen will ich das Gold.

LOGE

The Rhinemaidens	[4] Die Rheintöchter
called for your help:	riefen dich an:
so will you return them their treasure?	so dürfen Erhörung sie hoffen?

WOTAN

Stop your chatter!	Schweige, Schwätzer!
Freia, the fair one,	Freia, die gute,
Freia has to be rescued!	Freia gilt es zu lösen.

LOGE

As you command,	Wie du befiehlst,
down we shall go.	führ ich dich schnell
Choose your way:	steil hinab:
shall we descend through the Rhine?	steigen wir denn durch den Rhein?

WOTAN

Not through the Rhine!

Nicht durch den Rhein!

LOGE

Then follow my steps
through this smoky cleft:
and slip down there after me!

So schwingen wir uns
durch die Schwefelkluft.
Dort schlüpfe mit mir hinein!

He goes ahead and disappears sideways into a crevice, from which at once a sulphurous vapour rises. [13b]

WOTAN

You others wait
till evening falls:
the youth we're losing
I'll buy back again with the gold!

Ihr andern harrt
bis Abend hier:
verlorner Jugend
[6] erjag ich erlösendes Gold!

He descends through the crevice after Loge. The sulphurous steam emerging from it spreads across the entire stage and rapidly fills it with thick clouds. The remaining gods are already invisible.

DONNER

Fare you well, Wotan!

Fahre wohl, Wotan!

FROH

Good luck! Good luck!

Glück auf! Glück auf!

FRICKA

And soon return
to your sorrowing wife!

O kehre bald
zur bangenden Frau!

The sulphurous vapour darkens into completely black cloud, which ascends from below to above. This is then transformed into a solid, dark rocky crevice, moving continually upwards so as to give the impression that the stage is sinking deeper into the earth. An increasing clamour, as of forging, is heard on all sides. [13a, 13b, 7b, 5, 3, 6, 17, 11b]

Scene Three. *A distant dark red glow shines from various directions. A subterranean cavern, stretching further than the eye can reach, becomes visible. It seems to open on every side into narrow shafts. Alberich tugs Mime, who is screeching, by the ear out of a shaft at the side.*

ALBERICH

Hehe! hehe!
Come here! Come here!
Treacherous imp!
You will be pinched,
painfully pricked
if it's not ready,
flawlessly forged,
that helm I told you to make!

Hehe! hehe!
Hieher! hieher!
Tückischer Zwerg!
Tapfer gezwickt
sollst du mir sein,
schaffst du nicht fertig,
wie ich's bestellt,
zur Stund das feine Geschmeid!

MIME
(*howling*)

Ohe! Ohe!
Ow! Ow!
Leave me alone!
All's been done,
just as you asked;
I toiled away,
finished the work.
Only stop twisting my ear!

Ohe! Ohe!
Au! Au!
Lass mich nur los!
Fertig ist's,
wie du befahlst;
mit Fleiss und Schweiss
ist es gefügt:
nimm nur die Nägel vom Ohr!

ALBERICH
(*letting him go*)

Then why did you wait?
I want it now!

Was zögerst du dann
und zeigst es nicht?

69

I wasn't certain of every detail.	Ich Armer zagte, dass noch was fehle.

ALBERICH

And what is not finished?   Was wär' noch nicht fertig?

MIME
(*embarrassed*)

Here — and there —   Hier . . . und da.

ALBERICH

What 'here' and 'there'?   Was hier und da?
Give me the thing!   Her das Geschmeid!

He makes for Mime's ear again. Mime in his terror lets fall a piece of metalwork that he was clutching tightly in his hands. Alberich rapidly picks it up and examines it closely. [18]

Ha, you rogue!	Schau, du Schelm!
Everything's perfect	Alles geschmiedet
and carefully forged,	und fertig gefügt,
just as I asked!	wie ich's befahl!
But maybe the fool	So wollte der Tropf
thought he could trick me,	schlau mich betrügen,
and keep this wonderful	für sich behalten
work for himself —	das hehre Geschmeid,
work which my cunning	das meine List
had taught him to forge!	ihn zu schmieden gelehrt?
Villain, do I read your mind?	Kenn ich dich dummen Dieb?

He puts the metalwork on his head, as a 'Tarnhelm'. [18]

The helm fits on my head:	Dem Haupt fügt sich der Helm:
now will the spell do its work?	ob sich der Zauber auch zeigt?
'Night and darkness,	'Nacht und Nebel,
fade from sight!'	niemand gleich!'

His form disappears. In its place is seen a column of vapour.

Where am I, brother?   Siehst du mich, Bruder?

MIME
(*looks around in astonishment.*)

Where are you? You've gone from my sight.   Wo bist du? Ich sehe dich nicht.

ALBERICH
(*invisible*)

Then feel me instead,	So fühle mich doch,
you lazy rogue!	du fauler Schuft!
I'll teach you to steal from me!	Nimm das für dein Diebesgelüst!

MIME
(*screams, and writhes under the blows of a scourge, whose strokes can be heard though it is invisible.*)

Ohe! Ohe!	Ohe! Ohe!
Ow! Ow! Ow!	Au! Au! Au!

ALBERICH
(*laughing, invisible*)

Hahahahahaha!	Hahahahahaha!
I thank you, brother!	Hab Dank, du Dummer!
Your work was true and good.	Dein Werk bewährt sich gut.
Hoho! hoho!	Hoho! hoho!
Niblungs below,	Niblungen all,
bow down to Alberich!	neigt euch nun Alberich!
I shall be watching	Überall weilt er nun,
to see that you're working;	euch zu bewachen;
day and night	Ruh und Rast
you must be toiling,	ist euch zerronnen;
sweating to serve [6]	ihm müsst ihr schaffen,
your invisible lord,	wo nicht ihr ihn schaut;

who can watch you unseen and spy on his subjects! You are my slaves now for ever! Hoho! hoho! Hear me, I'm near — the Niblungs' great lord!	wo nicht ihr ihn gewahrt, seid seiner gewärtig: untertan seid ihr ihm immer! Hoho! hoho! Hört ihn, er naht: der Niblungen Herr!

The column of vapour disappears towards the back. Alberich's raging and scolding are heard receding into the distance. Screams and cries answer him, from further and further away, until at last they are inaudible. Mime has cowered down with pain. Wotan and Loge descend through a crevice. [17, 5x]

LOGE

Nibelheim here! The murky darkness is broken by fiery flashes!	[13a] Nibelheim hier: durch bleiche Nebel wie blitzen dort feurige Funken!

MIME

Ow! Ow! Ow!	[17] Au! Au! Au!

WOTAN

But what's that groan? Who lies at our feet?	Hier stöhnt es laut: was liegt im Gestein?

LOGE
(bends over Mime.)

What have we whimpering here?	Was Wunder wimmerst du hier?

MIME

Ohe! Ohe! Ow! Ow!	Ohe! Ohe! Au! Au!

LOGE

Hi, Mime! Cheerful dwarf! And what's the trouble with you?	Hei, Mime! Muntrer Zwerg! Was zwickt und zwackt dich denn so?

MIME

Leave me in quiet!	Lass mich in Frieden!

LOGE

That I'll do gladly. Not just that, but — help I'll offer you, Mime!	Das will ich freilich, und mehr noch, hör: helfen will ich dir, Mime!

With difficulty, he sets him on his feet.

MIME

What help for me? I must obey the commands of my brother, for he has made me his slave.	[19] Wer hälfe mir? Gehorchen muss ich dem leiblichen Bruder, der mich in Bande gelegt.

LOGE

But, Mime, what gave him the power to command?	Dich, Mime, zu binden, was gab ihm die Macht?

MIME

The Rhine's bright gold, seized by Alberich, was shaped and forged to a shining ring: at its magic spell the Nibelungs tremble; that ring makes him our master; we Niblungs are now his slaves.	[19] Mit arger List schuf sich Alberich aus Rheines Gold einen gelben Reif: [6] seinem starken Zauber zittern wir staunend; mit ihm zwingt er uns alle, der Niblungen nächt'ges Heer.

Once we were carefree,
worked at our anvils,
forged for our women
trinkets and jewels,
delicate Nibelung toys;
we merrily hammered away.
But now he compels us
to creep through the mineshafts;
for him alone
we sweat and we slave.
And the golden ring
has magical power
to show where treasure
lies hid in the rocks;
And then we must mine it,
forge and refine it
and smelt the ore down
to pure, shining gold;
so by day and night
we serve the greed of our lord.

[17] Sorglose Schmiede,
schufen wir sonst wohl
Schmuck unsern Weibern,
wonnig Geschmeid,
niedlichen Niblungentand,
wir lachten lustig der Müh.
Nun zwingt uns der Schlimme,
[5x] in Klüfte zu schlüpfen,
für ihn allein
uns immer zu mühn.
Durch des Ringes Gold
errät seine Gier,
wo neuer Schimmer
in Schachten sich birgt:
[4x] da müssen wir spähen,
spüren und graben,
die Beute schmelzen
[6] und schmieden den Guss,
ohne Ruh und Rast
[17] dem Herrn zu häufen den Hort.

LOGE

And you were so idle
that you were whipped?

Dich Trägen soeben
traf wohl sein Zorn?

MIME

Poor Mime, ah,
my fate was the hardest!
A magic helm
I had to make him;
he gave me detailed,
careful instructions.
And so I guessed
some wondrous spell
must lie in the work
that I forged so well;
I thought I'd keep
one thing for myself,
and use the spell
to free me from Alberich's power;
perhaps, yes, perhaps
the tyrant himself could be conquered;
by using the helm I might catch him.
That ring — could I but seize it,
then, though I'm forced now to serve him,
when free, I could make him my slave!

Mich Ärmsten, ach,
mich zwang er zum ärgsten:
[17, 18] ein Helmgeschmeid
hiess er mich schweissen;
genau befahl er,
wie es zu fügen.
Wohl merkt' ich klug,
welch mächt'ge Kraft
zu eigen dem Werk
das aus Erz ich wob:
für mich drum hüten
wollt' ich den Helm,
durch seinen Zauber
Alberichs Zwang mich entziehn —
vielleicht, ja vielleicht
den Lästigen selbst überlisten,
in meine Gewalt ihn zu werfen,
[6] den Ring ihm zu entreissen,
dass, wie ich Knecht jetzt dem Kühnen,
mir Freien er selber dann fröhn'!

LOGE

Your plan was clever;
why did it fail?

Warum, du Kluger,
glückte dir's nicht?

MIME

Ah! When the helm was finished,
the magic that makes it work,
that magic I could not guess right:
then he seized the helm
and spoke the charm;
he showed me — alas,
I learnt it too late —
mighty spells lay in that helm.
From my sight he vanished;
and out of the darkness
dealt invisible blows.

Ach, der das Werk ich wirkte,
[18] den Zauber, der ihn entzückt,
den Zauber erriet ich nicht recht!
Der das Werk mir riet
und mir's entriss,
der lehrte mich nun
— doch leider zu spät! —
welche List läg' in dem Helm:
meinem Blick entschwand er,
doch Schwielen dem Blinden
schlug unschaubar sein Arm.

(*howling and sobbing*)

| And that's all the thanks | Das schuf ich mir Dummen |
| my work has won! | schön zu Dank! |

He rubs his back. Wotan and Loge laugh. [6]

LOGE
(*to Wotan*)

| Admit, your task | Gesteh, nicht leicht |
| may well be hard. | gelingt der Fang. |

WOTAN

| We'll succeed at last, | | Doch erliegt der Feind, |
| thanks to your wits. | [13a] | hilft deine List. |

MIME
(*perplexed by the gods' laughter, observes them more closely.*)

| But why all these questions? | Mit eurem Gefrage, |
| Who are you, you strangers? | wer seid denn ihr Fremde? |

LOGE

Friends to you;	Freunde dir;
we can set free	von ihrer Not
the suffering Nibelung folk.	befrein wir der Niblungen Volk.

MIME
(*shrinks back in terror as he hears Alberich approaching.*) [17, 5x]

| Better take care; | Nehmt euch in acht! |
| Alberich's near. | Alberich naht. |

WOTAN

| We'll wait for him here. | [6] Sein harren wir hier. |

He seats himself calmly on a stone. Loge leans at his side. Alberich, brandishing a whip, enters, driving a team of Nibelungs in front of him out of a cavern lying further below. He has removed the Tarnhelm from his head and hung it from his belt. The Nibelungs are laden with gold and silver work, which, under Alberich's constant supervision, they pile up in a heap. [17, 5x]

ALBERICH

Hither! Thither!		Hieher! Dorthin!
Hehe! Hoho!		Hehe! Hoho!
Lazy herd!	[4]	Träges Heer,
Pile the gold		dort zu Hauf
there in a heap!		schichtet den Hort!
You there, get up!		Du da, hinauf!
On with your work!		Willst du voran?
Indolent dogs!		Schmähliches Volk,
Stack up the treasure!		ab das Geschmeide!
Want me to help you?		Soll ich euch helfen?
There in a heap!		Alles hieher!

He is suddenly aware of Wotan and Loge.

Hey, who is there?	He, wer ist dort?
Who's broken in?	Wer drang hier ein?
Mime, come here!	Mime! Zu mir,
Pestilent imp,	schäbiger Schuft!
chattering away	Schwatztest du gar
with that scoundrely pair!	mit dem schweifenden Paar?
Off, you idler!	Fort, du Fauler!
Back to your welding and whining!	Willst du gleich schmieden und schaffen?

He drives Mime with blows of his whip into the crowd of Nibelungs.

Hey! To your labour!	He, an die Arbeit!
Back to the forges!	Alle von hinnen!
Back to the mines!	Hurtig hinab!
From the new-dug shafts	Aus den neuen Schachten
go fetch me more gold!	schafft mir das Gold!

And if you're lazy
you shall be whipped.
Let no one be idle;
Mime will watch you
or else he will find
that my whip rewards him.
I'll be everywhere, spying
where no one expects;
ask Mime; he can explain!
Off to your work!
Lingering still?

Euch grüsst die Geissel,
grabt ihr nicht rasch!
Dass keiner mir müssig,
bürge mir Mime,
sonst birgt er sich schwer
meiner Geissel Schwunge:
dass ich überall weile,
wo keiner mich wähnt,
das weiss er, dünkt mich, genau!
Zögert ihr noch?
Zaudert wohl gar?

He draws the ring from his finger, kisses it, and holds it out threateningly. [6]

Tremble in terror,   [5]
you wretched slaves:
and obey
the ring's great lord!

Zittre und zage,
gezähmtes Heer:
rasch gehorcht
des Ringes Herrn!

With howling and shrieking the Nibelungs, Mime among them, scatter and scuttle away into the shafts. Alberich gives a long, suspicious look at Wotan and Loge. [6, 17]

What brought you here?

Was wollt ihr hier?

WOTAN

Of Nibelheim's dusky land
we've heard a most marvellous tale:
mighty wonders
worked here by Alberich;
and, eager to see them,
we arrive as your guests.

Von Nibelheims nächt'gem Land
vernahmen wir neue Mär:
mächt'ge Wunder
wirke hier Alberich:
daran uns zu weiden,
trieb uns Gäste die Gier.

ALBERICH

Attracted by   [13b]
Nibelheim's gold:
I know
the sort of guests that you are!

Nach Nibelheim
führt euch der Neid:
so kühne Gäste,
glaubt, kenn ich gut.

LOGE

Well, if you know,
impudent dwarf,
then say, who am I!
Why do you bark?
In chilly caves
you shivered and froze;
who gave you light
and who lit your fires then?
Was Loge not once your friend?
What use are your forges
till they are heated by me?
I am your kinsman   [13b]
and once was kind:
for that you owe me your thanks!

Kennst du mich gut,
kindischer Alp?
Nun sag: wer bin ich,
dass du so bellst?
Im kalten Loch,
da kauernd du lagst,
wer gab dir Licht
und wärmende Lohe,
wenn Loge nie dir gelacht?
Was hülf' dir dein Schmieden,
heizt' ich die Schmiede dir nicht?
Dir bin ich Vetter
und war dir Freund:
nicht fein drum dünkt mich dein Dank!

ALBERICH

The gods have
befriended Loge,
that crafty rogue:
are you, schemer, their friend,
as my friend once you were?
Haha! I laugh!
In that case, what need I fear?

Den Lichtalben
lacht jetzt Loge,
der list'ge Schelm:
bist du Falscher ihr Freund,
wie mir Freund du einst warst,
haha! mich freut's!
Von ihnen fürcht ich dann nichts.

LOGE

And so, instead, you can trust.

So denk ich, kannst du mir traun.

ALBERICH

I can trust your untruth,
never your truth!

Deiner Untreu trau ich,
nicht deiner Treu!

74

Yet today I can defy you!	(*assuming a defiant attitude*) Doch getrost trotz ich euch allen.

LOGE

Have you grown so daring and bold? Have you gained such mighty power?	[13b] Hohen Mut verleiht deine Macht: grimmig gross wuchs dir die Kraft.

ALBERICH

See all the gold that my slaves heaped over there?	Siehst du den Hort, den mein Heer dort mir gehäuft?

LOGE

I've never seen so much before.	So neidlichen sah ich noch nie.

ALBERICH

That's just today's — the merest trifle. In the future it will tower far more grandly.	[20] Das ist für heut, ein kärglich Häufchen: kühn und mächtig soll er künftig sich mehren.

WOTAN

But what's the use of your wealth? In joyless Nibelheim, with gold there's nothing to buy!	Zu was doch frommt dir der Hort, da freudlos Nibelheim und nichts für Schätze hier feil?

ALBERICH

Gold can be mined here, and gold can be stored here, deep in Nibelheim's caves. Then with my wealth from the darkness I'll rise, rise and be master of all things; the whole wide world I'll buy for myself with the treasure!	[5x] Schätze zu schaffen und Schätze zu bergen, nützt mir Nibelheims Nacht; [20] doch mit dem Hort, in der Höhle gehäuft, [6] denk ich dann Wunder zu wirken: die ganze Welt gewinn ich mit ihm mir zu eigen.

WOTAN

My good Niblung, how would you start?	Wie beginnst du, Gütiger, das?

ALBERICH

In the clouds, you great ones far above us may live, laugh, and love. My golden grasp will seize on you gods and destroy you! Once I renounced all joys of love. All those who live, all shall renounce them! Enchanted by gold, your greed for gold shall enslave you! On glorious heights you gods live in gladness, lulled by ease, despising those who work below, sure you are eternal! Beware! Beware! For first your men shall yield to my might, then your lovely women, who despise me and jeer, shall grant to Alberich's force what love could not win! Hahahaha!	Die in linder Lüfte Wehn da oben ihr lebt, [11a] lacht und liebt; mit goldner Faust euch Göttliche fang ich mir alle! [7a] Wie ich der Liebe abgesagt, alles, was lebt, [11a] soll ihr entsagen! Mit Golde gekirrt, nach Gold nur sollt ihr noch gieren. [8] Auf wonnigen Höhn in seligem Weben wiegt ihr euch; den Schwarzalben verachtet ihr ewigen Schwelger! Habt Acht! Habt Acht! Denn dient ihr Männer erst meiner Macht, eure schmucken Frau'n — die mein Frein verschmäht — sie zwingt zur Lust sich der Zwerg, lacht Liebe ihm nicht. Hahahaha!

You have been warned!
Beware!
Beware of my armies of night!
Beware the day when the Niblung's gold [5x]
shall vanquish the world!

Habt ihr's gehört?
[20] Habt Acht!
Habt Acht vor dem nächtlichen Heer,
entsteigt des Niblungen Hort
[3, 8b] aus stummer Tiefe zu Tag!

WOTAN
(*vehemently*)

No more, impious wretch!

Vergeh, frevelnder Gauch!

ALBERICH

What says he?   Was sagt der?

LOGE
(*stepping between them; to Wotan*)

Try to be patient!   Sei doch bei Sinnen!
(*to Alberich*)
All must stand in amazement,   [13a] Wen doch fasste nicht Wunder,
beholding Alberich's work!   erfährt er Alberichs Werk?
If only your craft can achieve   Gelingt deiner herrlichen List,
all that you plan with your treasure,   was mit dem Horte du heischest,
then all would acclaim you as master; [8b] den Mächtigsten muss ich dich rühmen:
the moon and stars,   denn Mond und Stern'
and the sun in his splendour,   und die strahlende Sonne,
how could they not obey you,   sie auch dürfen nicht anders,
serve you, bow to your will?   [8] dienen müssen sie dir.
But, most of all, it's important [17] Doch wichtig acht ich vor allem,
that your army of workers,   dass des Hortes Häufer,
your Nibelung slaves,   der Niblungen Heer,
never should rebel!   neidlos dir geneigt.
By your ring you can command;   [6] Einen Reif rührtest du kühn,
your people trembled in fear.   dem zagte zitternd dein Volk:
But, while you sleep,   [17] doch wenn im Schlaf
a thief might approach;   ein Dieb dich beschlich',
the ring he'd steal from your hand: den Ring schlau dir entriss',
so guard yourself, wise one, from that! [13a] wie wahrtest du, Weiser, dich dann?

ALBERICH

So no one is wise like Loge?   Der Listigste dünkt sich Loge;
He can see where   andre denkt er
others are blind?   immer sich dumm:
You give me a warning   dass sein ich bedürfte
and hope I'll beg   zu Rat und Dienst
for your advice.   um harten Dank,
Well, I do not need your help!   das hörte der Dieb jetzt gern!
This magical helm,   [18]   Den hehlenden Helm
invented by me,   ersann ich mir selbst;
was skilfully forged.   der sorglichste Schmied,
Mime made it to guard me.   Mime, musst' ihn mir schmieden:
It can transform me;   schnell mich zu wandeln
I can assume   nach meinem Wunsch,
any shape that I wish for,   die Gestalt mir zu tauschen,
through this helm.   taugt der Helm.
None can see me,   Niemand sieht mich,
search as he will;   wenn er mich sucht;
invisible master   doch überall bin ich,
and all-seeing lord!   geborgen dem Blick.
So I'm protected;   So ohne Sorge
even from you I am safe,   bin ich selbst sicher vor dir,
my kind, provident friend!   du fromm sorgender Freund!
[8b, 13a]

LOGE

Many marvels   Vieles sah ich,
I have encountered,   Seltsames fand ich:

76

but such a marvel
is new to me.
This work without equal —
I don't believe it!
If you could work this wonder,
then your power would be everlasting!

doch solches Wunder
gewahrt' ich nie.
Dem Werk ohnegleichen
kann ich nicht glauben;
wäre dies eine möglich,
deine Macht währte dann ewig.

ALBERICH

I do not lie
or boast like Loge!

Meinst du, ich lüg
und prahle wie Loge?

LOGE

Show me a proof,
and then I'll believe your boast.

Bis ich's geprüft,
bezweifl' ich, Zwerg, dein Wort.

ALBERICH

You're puffed up with prudence
and pride till you're bursting!
Well, envy me now!
Command, and tell me what shape
you would like me to be!

[17]   Vor Klugheit bläht sich
zum platzen der Blöde!
Nun plage dich Neid!
Bestimm, in welcher Gestalt
soll ich jach vor dir stehn?

LOGE

Oh, choose for yourself,
but make me dumb with surprise!

In welcher du willst:
nur mach vor Staunen mich stumm!

ALBERICH
(has put on the Tarnhelm.) [18]

'Dragon dread,
curling and coiling!'

'Riesen-Wurm
winde sich ringelnd!'

He disappears instantly. In his place an enormous dragon writhes on the ground; it rises up and snaps with open jaws at Wotan and Loge. [21]

LOGE
(pretends to be seized with terror.)

Ohe! Ohe!
Terrible dragon,
have mercy on me!
Spare my life, do not eat me!

Ohe! Ohe!
Schreckliche Schlange,
verschlinge mich nicht!
Schone Logen das Leben!

WOTAN

Hahaha! Good, Alberich!
Good, you rascal!
Your change from dwarf
to dragon was skilful and swift!

Hahaha! Gut, Alberich!
Gut, du Arger!
Wie wuchs so rasch
zum riesigen Wurme der Zwerg!

The dragon disappears. In its place, Alberich reappears in his own form.

ALBERICH

Hehe! You doubters!
Now do you believe?

Hehe! Ihr Klugen,
glaubt ihr mir nun?

LOGE

My trembling proves it too clearly!
A giant dragon
rose in your place;
now that I've seen,
how can I not believe you?
You can grow larger —
can you be tiny?
A tiny creature?
The safest way I know
to hide yourself from your foes.
That, maybe, would be hard?

Mein Zittern mag dir's bezeugen.
Zur grossen Schlange
schufst du dich schnell:
weil ich's gewahrt,
[8b, 13a] willig glaub ich dem Wunder.
Doch, wie du wuchsest,
kannst du auch winzig
und klein dich schaffen?
Das Klügste schien' mir das,
Gefahren schlau zu entfliehn:
das aber dünkt mich zu schwer!

77

Too hard for you,	Zu schwer dir,
ignorant fool!	weil du zu dumm!
How small shall I be?	Wie klein soll ich sein?

LOGE

So the smallest crack could conceal you,	Dass die feinste Klinze dich fasse,
where a frightened toad could be hid.	wo bang die Kröte sich birgt.

ALBERICH

Pah! That's easy!	Pah! nichts leichter!
Look at me now!	Luge du her!

He puts on the Tarnheim again. [18]

'Tiny toad,	'Krumm und grau
creeping and crawling!' —	krieche Kröte!'

He disappears; the gods see a toad on the rocks, creeping towards them.

LOGE
(to Wotan)

There, the toad!	Dort die Kröte,
Capture it quick!	greife sie rasch!

Wotan puts his foot on the toad. Loge catches it by the head and seizes the Tarnhelm in his hand.

ALBERICH
(suddenly becomes visible in his own form, writhing under Wotan's foot.)

Ohe! Ohe!	Ohe! Verflucht!
Now they have caught me!	Ich bin gefangen!

LOGE

Hold him tight,	Halt ihn fest,
till he is bound.	bis ich ihn band.

He has brought out a rope, and with it he binds Alberich hand and foot; then both seize the prisoner, who is violently trying to escape, and drag him to the shaft by which they entered.

Now swiftly up!	Schnell hinauf:
He is our prisoner!	dort ist er unser.

They disappear, climbing upwards. [8b, 13a]

Scene Four. *The scene changes as before, but in the opposite direction. The transformation again leads past the forging.* [6, 7b, 17, 11b, 12, 8b, 13a, 16a, 4x, 13b, 5x] *There is continual upward motion. Finally, there reappears the open space on a mountain height as in the second scene; but now it is veiled in thin mist, as at the end of Scene 2, after Freia's abduction. Wotan and Loge, bringing Alberich, bound, with the, come up out of the crevice.*

LOGE

There, Alberich,	Da, Vetter,
sit on your throne!	sitze du fest!
Look around you,	Luge, Liebster,
there lies the world	dort liegt die Welt,
that you thought you would rule as your own.	die du Lungrer gewinnen dir willst:
What spot for me	welch Stellchen, sag,
has been reserved in your realm?	bestimmst du drin mir zum Stall?

He dances round him, snapping his fingers. [13a]

ALBERICH

Infamous schemer!	Schändlicher Schächer!
You knave! You thief!	Du Schalk! Du Schelm!
Loosen my bonds,	Löse den Bast,
let me go free	binde mich los,
or else for your crime you will suffer!	den Frevel sonst büssest du Frecher!

78

You're now my captive,
bound in my fetters —
you who declared
you'd bind the world,
and lay it in chains before you;
my captive, bound at my feet.
I have you now at my mercy!
So if you'd be free,
then pay for your freedom.

Gefangen bist du,
fest mir gefesselt,
wie du die Welt,
was lebt und webt,
in deiner Gewalt schon wähntest,
in Banden liegst du vor mir.
Du Banger kannst es nicht leugnen!
Zu ledigen dich
bedarf's nun der Lösung.

ALBERICH

I was blind
and lost in my dreams!
A fool, caught by
that cowardly trick!
I shall have vengeance,
cruel and keen!

Oh, ich Tropf,
ich träumender Tor!
Wie dumm traut' ich
dem diebischen Trug!
Furchtbare Rache
räche den Fehl!

LOGE

Well, dream of your vengeance,
but first, set yourself free:
when a man's a captive,
no one cares if he curses.
Still planning your vengeance?
Better think quickly,
think of the ransom we need!

Soll Rache dir frommen,
vor allem rate dich frei:
dem gebundnen Manne
büsst kein Freier den Frevel.
Drum, sinnst du auf Rache,
rasch ohne Säumen
sorg um die Lösung zunächst!

Rubbing his fingers, he gives him to understand the kind of ransom.

ALBERICH
(*gruffly*)

Then say what you demand.

So heischt, was ihr begehrt!

WOTAN

The gold, all your shining gold.

Den Hort und dein helles Gold.

ALBERICH

Greedy and criminal pair!

But so long as I keep the ring,
the rest can be given away;
I can quickly replace it
again and again
by commanding the powerful ring.
Now a lesson I've learnt,
and wiser I'll be;
the warning is cheap at the price,
though it has cost me much gold.

[6] Gieriges Gaunergezücht!
(*aside*)
Doch behalt ich mir nur den Ring,
des Hortes entrat ich dann leicht:
denn von neuem gewonnen
und wonnig genährt
ist er bald durch des Ringes Gebot.
[19] Eine Witzigung wär's,
die weise mich macht:
zu teuer nicht zahl ich die Zucht,
lass für die Lehre ich den Tand.

WOTAN

You'll give me the gold?

Erlegst du den Hort?

ALBERICH

Loosen my hand;
I'll summon it here.

Löst mir die Hand,
so ruf ich ihn her.

Loge unties the rope from his right hand. Alberich puts the ring to his lips and secretly murmurs a command. [6, 5]

And now the Niblungs
will come to my call,
for their lord commands them;
up from the depths
of the darkness they'll bring you the gold:
so now set me free from my bonds!

[17] Wohlan, die Niblungen
rief ich mir nah:
[20] ihrem Herrn gehorchend
hör ich den Hort
aus der Tiefe sie führen zu Tag.
Nun löst mich vom lästigen Band!

Not yet, till all has been paid.   Nicht eh'r, bis alles gezahlt.

The Nibelungs ascend from the crevice, laden with the treasures of the hoard. During what
follows, they pile up the treasure. [17, 5x, 20]

ALBERICH

Oh, shameful disgrace,	O schändliche Schmach,
that my shrinking servants	dass die scheuen Knechte
should see me bound like a slave!	geknebelt selbst mich erschaun!

(to the Nibelungs)

Put it down there,	Dorthin geführt,
as I command!	wie ich's befehl!
In a heap	All zuhauf
pile up the gold!	schichtet den Hort!
Want me to help you?	Helf ich euch Lahmen?
No, don't look at me!	Hieher nicht gelugt!
Hurry! Quick!	Rasch da, rasch!
Then back to your labour!	Dann rührt euch von hinnen:
Off to the mines!	dass ihr mir schafft!
Off to the forges!	Fort in die Schachten!
Idlers, back to your work!	Weh euch, find ich euch faul!
For your lord comes hard on your heels! [5]	Auf den Fersen folg ich euch nach.

He kisses his ring and stretches it out commandingly. As if struck by a blow, the Nibelungs
hurry in fear and trembling to the crevice and quickly scuttle down it.

The gold lies there;		Gezahlt hab ich:
now let me go:		nun lasst mich ziehn!
and the Tarnhelm there,	[18]	Und das Helmgeschmeid,
which Loge still holds,		das Loge dort hält
now kindly return it to me!		das gebt mir nun gütlich zurück!

LOGE
(throwing the Tarnhelm on to the hoard)

The Tarnhelm is part of the ransom.   Zur Busse gehört auch die Beute.

ALBERICH

Accursed thief!	[6]	Verfluchter Dieb!
Yet, wait a while!		Doch nur Geduld!
He who forged me the first		Der den alten mir schuf,
can make me another.		schafft einen andern:
I still hold the power		noch halt ich die Macht,
that Mime obeys.		der Mime gehorcht.
Yet it's sad	[19]	Schlimm zwar ist's,
that crafty foes		dem schlauen Feind
should capture my cunning defence!		zu lassen die listige Wehr!
Well then! Alberich's	[18]	Nun denn! Alberich
paid his ransom;		liess euch alles:
untie, you tyrants, my bonds!		jetzt löst, ihr Bösen, das Band!

LOGE
(to Wotan)

Are you contented?	Bist du befriedigt?
Can he go free?	Bind ich ihn frei?

WOTAN

A golden ring	Ein goldner Ring
shines on your finger:	ragt dir am Finger:
well, my dwarf,	hörst du, Alp?
that also is part of the price.	Der, acht ich, gehört mit zum Hort.

ALBERICH
(appalled)

The ring?   Der Ring?

WOTAN

To win your freedom	Zu deiner Lösung
you'll have to yield it.	musst du ihn lassen.

My life, but not the ring!

The ring surrender:
with your life, do what you will!

But if my life is spared me,
the ring must stay on my finger:
hand and head,
eye and ear
are not mine more truly
than mine this golden ring!

What right have you to the ring?
Insolent, impudent Niblung?
Tell me now,
where did you get the gold
from which you created the ring?
Did you own it,
when you grasped it,
the Rhinemaids' radiant toy?
Let those Rhinemaids answer:
will they declare
that they gave you
their gold as a present;
or did you seize it by theft?

Infamous schemer!
Shameful deceit!
Thief, you blame me
for doing that crime
which you were burning to do!
Though you lusted
to steal the gold for yourself,
you couldn't pay
the price that alone would suffice.
It serves you well,
you smooth, sneering rogue,
that the Nibelung, I,
in shameful distress,
in a frenzied outburst,
did win for myself, by a curse,
this gold that smiles on you now!
And my sacrifice,
all I suffered,
my criminal,
curse-laden deed —
have they merely served
to procure you a plaything?
Will you win the world by my curse?
Guard yourself,
proud, cruel god!
If I have sinned,
I sinned but against myself:
but against all that was,
is, and shall be,
you are planning a crime
by laying your hand on the ring!

ALBERICH
(*trembling*)
Das Leben — doch nicht den Ring!

WOTAN
(*more violently*)
Den Reif verlang ich:
mit dem Leben mach, was du willst!

ALBERICH
Lös ich mir Leib und Leben,
den Ring auch muss ich mir lösen:
Hand und Haupt,
Aug und Ohr,
sind nicht mehr mein Eigen
als hier dieser rote Ring!

WOTAN
Dein Eigen nennst du den Ring?
Rasest du, schamloser Albe?
Nüchtern sag,
wem entnahmst du das Gold,
daraus du den schimmernden schufst?
War's dein Eigen,
was du Arger
der Wassertiefe entwandt?
[4x]   Bei des Rheines Töchtern
hole dir Rat,
ob ihr Gold sie
zu eigen dir gaben,
das du zum Ring dir geraubt.

ALBERICH
Schmähliche Tücke,
schändlicher Trug!
Wirfst du Schächer
die Schuld mir vor,
die dir so wonnig erwünscht?
[6]   Wie gern raubtest
du selbst dem Rheine das Gold,
war nur so leicht
die List, es zu schmieden, erlangt?
Wie glückt' es nun
dir Gleissner zum Heil,
dass der Niblung ich
aus schmählicher Not,
in des Zornes Zwange,
den schrecklichen Zauber gewann,
dess' Werk nun lustig dir lacht!
Des Unseligsten,
Angstversehrten
fluchfertige,
furchtbare Tat,
zu fürstlichem Tand
soll sie fröhlich dir taugen,
zur Freude dir frommen mein Fluch?
[6]   Hüte dich,
herrischer Gott!
Frevelte ich,
so frevelt' ich frei an mir:
doch an allem, was war,
ist und wird,
frevelst, Ewiger, du,
entreissest du frech mir den Ring!

81

	WOTAN
Yield the ring!	[9a] Her den Ring!
No chatter can prove	Kein Recht an ihm
your right to the ring!	schwörst du schwatzend dir zu.

He seizes Alberich and violently tears the ring from his finger. [3]

ALBERICH
(*with a terrible cry*)

Ha! Defeated! And tricked!	[6] Ha! Zertrümmert! Zerknickt!
Of wretches, the wretchedest slave!	[7b] Der Traurigen traurigster Knecht!

WOTAN
(*contemplating the ring*)

It shines there,lifts me on high,	Nun halt ich, was mich erhebt,
of mighty ones, mightiest of all!	der Mächtigen mächtigsten Herrn!

He puts on the ring. [6]

LOGE

Can he be freed?	Ist er gelöst?

WOTAN

Set him free!	Bind ihn los!

LOGE
(*frees Alberich from his bonds.*)

Slip away home!	Schlüpfe denn heim!
Not a fetter holds you:	Keine Schlinge hält dich:
free, Alberich, free!	frei fahre dahin!

ALBERICH
(*raising himself*) [22]

Am I now free?	Bin ich nun frei?
Truly free?	Wirklich frei?
I greet you then	So grüss' euch denn
in my freedom: mark my words!	meiner Freiheit erster Gruss!
Since a curse gained it for me,	[23] Wie durch Flucht er mir geriet,
my curse lies on this ring!	verflucht sei dieser Ring!
Though its gold	Gab sein Gold
brought riches to me,	mir Macht ohne Mass,
let now it bring	nun zeug' sein Zauber
but death, death to its lord!	Tod dem, der ihn trägt!
Its wealth shall yield	Kein Froher soll
pleasure to none;	seiner sich freun;
let no fortunate owner	keinem Glücklichen lache
enjoy its gleam.	sein lichter Glanz!
Care shall consume	[22] Wer ihn besitzt,
the man who commands it,	den sehre die Sorge,
and mortal envy	und wer ihn nicht hat,
consume those who don't —	den nage der Neid!
striving vainly	Jeder giere
to win that prize.	nach seinem Gut,
But he who obtains it	doch keiner geniesse
shall find no joy!	mit Nutzen sein!
It will bring no gain to its lord;	Ohne Wucher hüt' ihn sein Herr,
only death is brought by its gleam!	[23] doch den Würger zieh' er ihm zu!
To death he is fated,	Dem Tode verfallen,
doomed by the curse on the ring:	fessle den Feigen die Furcht;
and while he lives,	solang er lebt,
fears will fill all his days.	sterb' er lechzend dahin,
Who owns the ring	des Ringes Herr
to the ring is a slave,	[5x] als des Ringes Knecht:
till the gold returns	bis in meiner Hand
to this hand from which you have torn it!	den geraubten wieder ich halte!

In anguish and sore distress, the Nibelung blesses the ring! You hold it now; guard it with care! From my curse you can't escape!	So segnet in höchster Not der Nibelung seinen Ring! Behalt ihn nun, hüte ihn wohl, meinem Fluch fliehest du nicht!

He disappears quickly into the crevice. The thick mists in the foreground gradually clear.
[5x, 4x]

LOGE

Did you hear Alberich's loving song?	Lauschtest du seinem Liebesgruss?

WOTAN
(*lost in contemplation of the ring on his finger*)

Let him give way to his wrath!	Gönn ihm die geifernde Lust!

It continues to get lighter.

LOGE
(*looking offstage to the right*)

Fasolt and Fafner, coming this way! Freia shall soon be freed.	Fasolt und Fafner nahen von fern; Freia führen sie her.

Through the mists, as they continue to disperse, Donner, Froh, and Fricka appear and hasten towards the foreground. [16a]

FROH

So you have returned!	Sie kehrten zurück.

DONNER

Be welcome, brother!	Willkommen, Bruder!

FRICKA
(*to Wotan, anxiously*)

Have you gained the ransom?	[22] Bringst du gute Kunde?

LOGE
(*points to the treasure.*)

By cunning and force the deed was done: behold, there's Freia's price.	Mit List und Gewalt gelang das Werk: dort liegt, was Freia löst.

DONNER

From the giants' power soon we can free her.	Aus der Riesen Haft naht dort die Holde.

FROH

How sweetly the air charms us again; joy and contentment steal through my heart! Life indeed would be wretched if we were parted from her; she brings us youth eternal, fills us with joy and delight.	Wie liebliche Luft wieder uns weht, wonnig Gefühl die Sinne erfüllt! Traurig ging es uns allen, getrennt für immer von ihr, die leidlos ewiger Jugend jubelnde Lust uns verleiht.

The foreground is now completely clear again. The appearances of the gods have regained their former freshness. The veil of mist still hovers over the background, however, so that the castle remains invisible. Fasolt and Fafner enter, bringing Freia between them.

FRICKA
(*hastens joyfully to her sister, to embrace her.*)

Loveliest sister!	Lieblichste Schwester,

Sweetest delight!
Now once again I can greet you.

süsseste Lust!
Bist du mir wiedergewonnen?

FASOLT
(*restraining her*) [12]

Wait! Don't touch her yet!
Freia still is ours.
On Riesenheim's
far rocky heights,
there we did rest;
we guarded her
and we kept our word
faithfully.
Though sore at heart,
I now return her;
so keep your bargain
and pay our wage.

Halt! Nicht sie berührt!
Noch gehört sie uns.
Auf Riesenheims
ragender Mark
rasteten wir:
mit treuem Mut
des Vertrages Pfand
pflegten wir.
So sehr mich's reut,
zurück doch bring ich's,
[15] erlegt uns Brüdern
die Lösung ihr.

WOTAN

Behold, there's the ransom:
the golden heap
will reward you most generously.

Bereit liegt die Lösung:
des Goldes Mass
sei nun gütlich gemessen.

FASOLT

To lose the woman
sorely distresses my heart.
If I am forced to forget her,
you must pile the gold,
heap up the hoard,
till you conceal
her beauty and charms from my sight.

Das Weib zu missen,
wisse, gemutet mich weh:
[11a] soll aus dem Sinn sie mir schwinden,
des Geschmeides Hort
häufet denn so,
dass meinem Blick
[7b] die Blühende ganz er verdeck'!

WOTAN

Then heap the gold
till Freia is hid.

So stellt das Mass
nach Freias Gestalt.

The two giants place Freia in the middle. [11] *Then they thrust their staves in the ground on each side of Freia, so as to measure her height and breadth.* [12, 15]

FAFNER

We've planted our poles here
to frame her form;
now heap your gold to her height!

Gepflanzt sind die Pfähle
nach Pfandes Mass:
gehäuft nun füll es der Hort.

WOTAN

On with the work:
oh, this is shameful!

[11b] Eilt mit dem Werk:
widerlich ist mir's!

LOGE

Help me, Froh!

Hilf mir, Froh!

FROH

Freia's shame
soon shall be ended.

Freias Schmach
eil ich zu enden.

Loge and Froh quickly pile up the treasure between the staves. [15, 17]

FAFNER

Far too loose
you're piling the gold.

Nicht so leicht
und locker gefügt!

Roughly, he presses the treasure together tightly. [12, 17]

Firm and hard,
pack it tight!

Fest und dicht
füll er das Mass!

He stoops down to look for crevices. [20, 17]

Look, here is a chink:
and stop up this crevice!

Hier lug ich noch durch:
verstopft mir die Lücken!

84

Stand back, you ruffian! —

LOGE

Zurück, du Grober!

FAFNER

Look here!

Hierher!

LOGE

Off with your hands!

Greif mir nichts an!

FAFNER

And here! This crack must be closed!

ierher! Die Klinze verklemmt!

WOTAN
(*turning away in dejection*)

Deep in my breast
burns the disgrace!

[11b] Tief in der Brust
brennt mir die Schmach.

FRICKA
(*her eyes fixed on Freia*)

See where she stands;
how can she bear this shame?
And the glorious maid
pleads in silence for help.
Heartless man!
For you she endures this disgrace!

Sieh, wie in Scham
schmählich die Edle steht:
[11] um Erlösung fleht
stumm der leidende Blick.
Böser Mann!
Der Minnigen botest du das!

FAFNER

Still more! Heap on some more!

[12, 17]Noch mehr! Noch mehr hierher!

DONNER

I'll stand no more;
furious rage
rouses my heart to revenge!
Come here, you cur!
If you'd measure,
then try your measure with me!

Kaum halt ich mich:
schäumende Wut
weckt mir der schamlose Wicht!
Hieher, du Hund!
Willst du messen,
so miss dich selber mit mir!

FAFNER

Patience, Donner!
Roar where it helps:
but here you thunder in vain!

Ruhig, Donner!
Rolle, wo's taugt:
hier nützt dein Rasseln dir nichts!

DONNER
(*preparing to strike*)

Not in vain, since it can crush you!

Nicht dich Schmählichen zu
zerschmettern?

WOTAN

Patience, friend!
I think that Freia is hid!

Friede doch!
[15] Schon dünkt mich Freia verdeckt.

LOGE

The gold runs out.

[20] Der Hort ging auf.

FAFNER
(*measures the gold closely with his eye, looking for crevices.*) [16a]

But still I can see her hair!
You have some gold —
add it to the pile.

Noch schimmert mir Holdas Haar:
dort das Gewirk
wirf auf den Hort!

LOGE

What? Not the helm?

Wie, auch den Helm?

FAFNER

Quickly, give it us.

[18] Hurtig her mit ihm!

85

	WOTAN
Give them the Tarnhelm!	Lass ihn denn fahren!

LOGE

(*throws the Tarnhelm on the pile.*)

At last we have finished!	So sind wir denn fertig.
Are you contented?	Seid ihr zufrieden?

FASOLT

Freia, the fair one,	Freia, die schöne,
see I no more:	schau ich nicht mehr:
The ransom is paid?	so ist sie gelöst?
Fasolt must lose her?	Muss ich sie lassen?

He goes up close and peers through the pile. [20, 11]

Ah! Her glance	Weh! Noch blizt
still pierces my heart;	ihr Blick zu mir her;
her eyes like stars	des Auges Stern
shine on me still,	strahlt mich noch an:
for through this crack	durch eine Spalte
I look on their light.	[11] muss ich's erspähn!
I cannot turn from this maiden,	Seh ich dies wonnige Auge,
while her eyes inspire me with love.	von dem Weibe lass ich nicht ab.

FAFNER

Hey! I charge you,	He! Euch rat ich,
now stop up this crevice!	verstopft mir die Ritze!

LOGE

Never contented!	Nimmersatte!
Surely you see	Seht ihr denn nicht,
our gold's at an end?	ganz schwand uns der Hort?

FAFNER

Not wholly, friend!	Mit nichten, Freund!
On Wotan's finger	An Wotans Finger
gleams the gold of a ring:	glänzt von Gold noch ein Ring,
and that will fill up this crevice!	den gebt, die Ritze zu füllen!

WOTAN

What? Give my ring?	Wie! Diesen Ring?

LOGE

Just a moment!	[4x] Lasst euch raten!
The Rhinemaidens	Den Rheintöchtern
must have that gold,	gehört dies Gold:
and to them Wotan will give it.	ihnen gibt Wotan es wieder.

WOTAN

What chatter is this?	Was schwatzest du da?
This prize that I have won me,	Was schwer ich mir erbeutet,
without fear I'll keep for myself!	ohne Bangen wahr ich's für mich.

LOGE

But then how will I	[3] Schlimm dann steht's
keep the promise	um mein Versprechen,
I gave those sorrowful maids!	das ich den Klagenden gab.

WOTAN

What you promised is nothing to me:	Dein Versprechen bindet mich nicht:
I took the ring for myself.	als Beute bleibt mir der Reif.

FAFNER

And now you'll yield it,	[6] Doch hier zur Lösung
paying the ransom.	musst du ihn legen.

86

Freely ask what you want; all I shall grant you; but for the world I will not surrender the ring!	Fordert frech, was ihr wollt: alles gewähr ich, um alle Welt doch nicht fahren lass ich den Ring!

FASOLT
(angrily pulling Freia out from behind the pile)

Keep your gold, and keep your ring; and we'll keep Freia for ever!	Aus dann ist's, beim Alten bleibt's: nun folgt uns Freia für immer!

FREIA

Help me! Help me!	[5x]	Hilfe! Hilfe!

FRICKA

Cruel god! Do what they ask!	Harter Gott, gib ihnen nach!

FROH

Pay them the ransom!	Spare das Gold nich!

DONNER

Give them the ring too!	Spende den Ring doch!

Fafner restrains Fasolt, who is making off. All stand perplexed.

WOTAN

Leave me in peace! The ring stays with me!	Lasst mich in Ruh! Den Reif geb ich nicht.

Wotan turns angrily away. The stage has again become dark. A bluish light breaks from the rocky cleft at the side, and in it Erda suddenly appears, rising from below to half her height. Her noble features are ringed by a mass of black hair. [24]

ERDA
(stretching out her hand to Wotan in warning)

Yield it, Wotan, yield it! Yield the accursed ring! Wretchedness, doom and disaster lie there in the ring.	Weiche, Wotan, weiche! Flieh des Ringes Fluch! Rettungslos dunklem Verderben weiht dich sein Gewinn.

WOTAN

Who brings this warning of doom?	Wer bist du, mahnendes Weib?

ERDA

All of the past, know I. All things that are, all things that shall be — all I know: the endless world's all-wise one, Erda, bids you beware. My three daughters, born in Erda's primeval womb, shape my visions, tell you each night of the future. Today I myself, drawn by dread, come to advise. Hear me! Hear me! Hear me! All things that are, perish! An evil day	[24] [1b] [22] [5x] [24] [25]	Wie alles war, weiss ich; wie alles wird, wie alles sein wird, seh ich auch: der ew'gen Welt Ur-Wala, Erda mahnt deinen Mut. Drei der Töchter, ur-erschaffne, gebar mein Schoss: was ich sehe, sagen dir nächtlich die Nornen. Doch höchste Gefahr führt mich heut selbst zu dir her: Höre! Höre! Höre! Alles, was ist, endet, Ein düsterer Tag

dawns for the immortals: | dämmert den Göttern:
I warn you, yield up the ring! | [6] dir rat ich, meide den Ring!

Erda sinks slowly to breast level, as the bluish glow begins to fade. [24]

WOTAN

Mysterious doom | Geheimnis-hehr
sounds in your words: | hallt mir dein Wort:
stay here, and warn me further! | weile, dass mehr ich wisse!

ERDA
(*disappearing*) [24]

You heard my words; | Ich warnte dich —
you know enough: | du weisst genug: '
brood in dread and fear! | sinn in Sorg und Furcht!

She disappears completely.

WOTAN

But if dread will torment me, | Soll ich sorgen und fürchten —
then I must hold you; | [5x] dich muss ich fassen,
all you must tell me! | alles erfahren!

He tries to follow and stop her as she disappears into the crevice. Froh and Fricka throw themselves in his way and hold him back.

FRICKA

Be careful, calm yourself! | Was willst du, Wütender?

FROH

Be wise, Wotan! | Halt ein, Wotan!
Erda is holy; | Scheue die Edle,
do as she says! | achte ihr Wort!

Wotan gazes thoughtfully before him. [24]

DONNER
(*turning decisively to the giants*)

Hear, you giants! | Hört, ihr Riesen!
Come back, be patient! | Zurück und harret:
The gold, Wotan will give you. | das Gold wird euch gegeben.

FREIA

Ah, dare I hope it? | Darf ich es hoffen?
Is your Freia | Dünkt euch Holda
worth such a great reward? | wirklich der Lösung wert?

All look eagerly at Wotan. [24] *After thinking deeply, he rouses himself, seizes his spear and brandishes it as the sign of a bold decision.* [9a]

WOTAN

To me, Freia! | Zu mir, Freia!
You shall be freed. | Du bist befreit.
Bought with the gold, | Wiedergekauft
bring us our youth once again! | [7b] kehr uns die Jugend zurück!
You giants, there is your ring! | Ihr Riesen, nehmt euren Ring!

He throws the ring on the pile. The giants release Freia. She hurries happily over to the gods, who spend some time embracing her in turn with the utmost delight. Meanwhile Fafner has spread out an enormous sack, and prepare to stow the hoard in it, to take it away.

FASOLT
(*intercepting his brother*) [12, 17]

Stop, you greedy one! | Halt, du Gieriger!
What about my share? | Gönne mir auch was!
Fairly and squarely | Redliche Teilung
we'll divide it. | taugt uns beiden.

88

You'd set your heart on the maid.
What do you care for the gold?
You hoped for love
and I wanted riches;
if you had won her,
would you have shared her with me?
Since it's the gold,
trust me to seize
on the greater part for myself!

FAFNER

Mehr an der Maid als am Gold
lag dir verliebtem Geck:
mit Müh zum Tausch
vermocht' ich dich Toren.
Ohne zu teilen,
hättest du Freia gefreit:
[5x] teil ich den Hort,
billig behalt ich
die grösste Hälfte für mich.

Shame on you, thief!
Mocking me so!
You gods be the judges:
how should this gold
be shared into two?

FASOLT

[5x] Schändlicher du!
Mir diesen Schimpf?
Euch ruf ich zu Richtern:
teilet nach Recht
uns redlich den Hort!

Wotan turns contemptuously away.

LOGE
(*to Fasolt*)

Let him keep the treasure;
all that you need is the ring!

[22] Den Hort lass ihn raffen:
halte du nur auf den Ring!

FASOLT
(*hurls himself upon Fafner, who has been busily packing away.*) [6]

Stand back, you robber!
Mine is the ring;
I won it for Freia's glance!

Zurück, du Frecher!
Mein ist der Ring;
mir blieb er für Freias Blick.

He snatches hastily at the ring. They struggle.

FAFNER

Off with your hands!
The ring is mine!

Fort mit der Faust!
Der Ring ist mein!

Fasolt wrests the ring from Fafner.

FASOLT

I have it, I shall keep it!

Ich halt ihn, mir gehort er!

FAFNER
(*striking out with his staff*)

Hold it fast, else it may fall!   Halt ihn fest, dass er nicht fall'!
He fells Fasolt with a single blow and then wrenches the ring from the dying giant.
Now dream of your Freia's glance!   Nun blinzle nach Freias Blick.
For the ring you'll see no more!   [6] an den Reif rührst du nicht mehr!

*He puts the ring in the sack, and then calmly finishes packing the treasure. All the gods are
appalled. A long, sudden silence.* [23]

WOTAN

Fearful power
lies held in that fatal curse!

Furchtbar nun
erfind ich des Fluchtes Kraft!

LOGE

Your luck, Wotan,
what could surpass it?
Much you gained from
the ring and the gold;
but that now you have lost them,
that's better still:
for your enemies, see,
murder each other
for the gold that you let go.

[22] Was gleicht, Wotan,
wohl deinem Glücke?
Viel erwarb dir
des Ringes Gewinn;
dass er nun dir genommen,
nützt dir noch mehr:
[12] deine Feinde — sieh,
fällen sich selbst
um das Gold, das du vergabst.

89

WOTAN
(profoundly agitated) [6]

Dark forebodings oppress me!		Wie doch Bangen mich bindet!
Fear and dread		Sorg und Furcht
seize on my soul.	[24]	fesseln den Sinn;
Erda can teach me		wie sie zu enden,
how I can end them:		lehre mich Erda:
to her, I must descend!		zu ihr muss ich hinab!

FRICKA
(caressing him, cajolingly) [10]

What keeps you, Wotan?		Wo weilst du, Wotan?
See where our home		Winkt dir nicht hold
awaits you there,	[8b]	die hehre Burg,
shining and glorious,		die des Gebieters
glad to welcome its lord.		gastlich bergend nun harrt?

WOTAN
(gloomily)

An evil wage	[6]	Mit bösem Zoll
paid for the work!	[23]	zahlt' ich den Bau!

DONNER
(pointing to the background, which is still wreathed in mist)

Sweltering mists	Schwüles Gedünst
hang in the air;	schwebt in der Luft;
I'm oppressed	lästig ist mir
by their gloomy weight.	der trübe Druck:
I'll gather the clouds,	das bleiche Gewölk
summon the lightning and thunder	samml' ich zu blitzendem Wetter;
to sweep the mist from the sky!	das fegt den Himmel mir hell.

He climbs onto a high rock by the precipice and there swings his hammer. Mists gather around him.

Heda! Heda! Hedo!	[26]	Heda! Heda! Hedo!
Now come to my call!		Zu mir, du Gedüft!
You vapours, to me!		Ihr Dünste, zu mir!
Donner, your lord,		Donner, der Herr,
summons you here!		ruft euch zu Heer.
As my hammer swings,		Auf des Hammers Schwung
sweep from the sky!		schwebet herbei:
Vapours and cloud!		dunstig Gedämpf,
Wandering fog!		schwebend Gedüft!
Donner, your lord, summons you here!		Donner, der Herr, ruft euch zu Heer!
Heda! Heda! Hedo!		Heda! Heda! Hedo!

Donner vanishes completely behind a thundercloud which grows ever thicker and blacker. His hammer-blow is heard striking hard on the rock. A large flash of lightning shoots from the cloud, followed by a violent clap of thunder. Froh has vanished with him into the cloud.

Brother, to me!	Bruder, hieher!
Show them the bridge to the hall.	Weise der Brücke den Weg!

Suddenly the clouds lift. Donner and Froh are visible. From their feet a rainbow bridge of blinding radiance stretches across the valley back to the castle, which now glows in the rays of the evening sun. Fafner has at last collected up all the treasure lying near his brother's corpse, put the enormous sack on his back, and left the stage during Donner's conjuration of the storm.

FROH
(to the gods, indicating with outstretched hand the bridge as the way across the valley)

The bridge leads you homeward,	Zur Burg führt die Brücke,
light, yet firm to your feet:	leicht, doch fest eurem Fuss:
so boldly tread	beschreitet kühn
on that shining path!	ihren schrecklosen Pfad!

Wotan and the other gods are lost in speechless astonishment at the glorious sight. [8]

Evening rays flood		Abendlich strahlt
the sky with splendour;		der Sonne Auge;
those glorious beams		in prächt'ger Glut
shine there on my hall.		prangt glänzend die Burg.
In the morning radiance		In des Morgens Scheine
bravely it glistened,		mutig erschimmernd,
standing masterless,		lag sie herrenlos
proud, awaiting its lord.		hehr verlockend vor mir.
From morning till evening,	[6]	Von Morgen bis Abend
in fear and dread,		in Müh und Angst
I worked dark deeds till I'd gained it!		nicht wonnig ward sie gewonnen!
The night is near:	[24]	Es naht die Nacht:
from all its ills		vor ihrem Neid
we have our refuge now.		biete sie Bergung nun.

(*very resolutely, as if seized by a grand thought*) [27]

So greet I the hall,	So grüss ich die Burg,
safe from all fear and dread.	sicher vor Bang und Graun!

He turns solemnly to Fricka.

Follow me, wife:	Folge mir, Frau:
in Walhall, reign there with me!	in Walhall wohne mit mir!

What name did you call it?	[8]	Was deutet der Name?
No name that I've ever heard of.		Nie, dünkt mich, hört' ich ihn nennen.

When all that I've dreamed	Was, mächtig der Furcht,
and planned comes to pass,	mein Mut mir erfand,
when victory is mine,	wenn siegend es lebt,
you'll understand that name!	leg es den Sinn dir dar!

He takes Fricka by the hand and with her strides slowly towards the bridge. Froh, Freia and Donner follow.

(*remaining in the foreground and looking back at the gods*) [13a, 6, 8a]

They are hastening on to their end,		Ihrem Ende eilen sie zu,
though they think they are great in their		die so stark im Bestehen sich wähnen.
grandeur.		
Ashamed I'd be		Fast schäm ich mich,
to share in their dealings;		mit ihnen zu schaffen;
I feel a temptation		zur leckenden Lohe
to turn and destroy them;		mich wieder zu wandeln,
change to flickering fire,		spür ich lockende Lust.
and burn those great ones		Sie aufzuzehren,
who thought I was tamed,	[13b]	die einst mich gezähmt,
rather than blindly		statt mit den Blinden
sink with the blind,		blöd zu vergehn,
although they're so gracious and god-like!		und wären es göttlichste Götter!
I think that might be best!		Nicht dumm dünkte mich das!
I must consider:		Bedenken will ich's:
who knows what I'll do?		wer weiss, was ich tu!

He goes nonchalantly to join the gods. [8c] *The singing of the Rhinemaidens is heard rising up from below.*

(*from the depths of the valley, invisible*)

Rhinegold! Rhinegold!	[1c, 4b]	Rheingold! Rheingold!
Shining gold!		Reines Gold!
How brightly and clear		Wie lauter und hell
glittered your beams on us!		leuchtest hold du uns!
For your true radiance		Um dich, du klares,
we are mourning;		wir nun klagen!

| give us the gold! | Gebt uns das Gold! |
| Oh, give us its glory again. | O gebt uns das reine zurück! |

WOTAN
(*in the act of setting foot on the bridge, pauses and turns round.*)

| What cries arise from the deep? | [3] Welch Klagen klingt zu mir her? |

LOGE
(*looking down into the valley*)

| The mournful Rhinemaidens | Des Rheines Kinder |
| cry for their stolen gold. | beklagen des Goldes Raub. |

WOTAN

| Accursed nixies! | Verwünschte Nicker! |
| Stop their tiresome lament! | Wehre ihrem Geneck! |

LOGE
(*calling down into the valley*) [8b]

You in the water,	Ihr da im Wasser,
stop wailing to us.	was weint ihr herauf?
Hear what Wotan decrees.	Hört, was Wotan euch wünscht.
Never more	Glanzt nicht mehr
will you see your gold;	euch Mädchen das Gold,
let the gods' new golden splendour	in der Götter neuem Glanze
shine upon you instead!	sonnt euch selig fortan!

The gods laugh and stride on to the bridge. [13a]

THE RHINEMAIDENS
(*from below*)

Rhinegold! Rhinegold!	[1c, 4b] Rheingold! Rheingold!
Shining gold!	Reines Gold!
Return to the deep,	O leuchtete noch
let us bathe in your light again!	[3] in der Tiefe dein lautrer Tand!
Goodness and truth	Traulich und treu
dwell but in the waters:	ist's nur in der Tiefe:
false and base	falsch und feig
all those who dwell up above!	ist, was dort oben sich freut!

While the gods are crossing the bridge to the castle, the curtain falls. [8b, 27]

Contributors

John Deathridge is a lecturer in Music at Cambridge University and a Fellow of King's College.

Roger North has composed orchestral, chamber, choral, operatic and electro-acoustic works. He has given many broadcast talks and has lately turned to writing on music. A detailed musical analysis of *Tristan and Isolde* is in preparation. He is a tutor at Morley College.

Stewart Spencer is a Lecturer in German at Royal Holloway and Bedford New College, University of London, and editor of the Wagner Society's quarterly journal *Wagner*.

The entrance of the gods into Valhalla, San Francisco, 1985 (photo: William Acheson)

Selective Discography *by Cathy Peterson*

Conductor Orchestra/ Opera House Date	*W. Furtwängler* **Rome PO** *1953*	*G. Solti* **Vienna PO** *1958*	*K. Böhm* **Bayreuth Festival** *1966*	*H. von Karajan* **Berlin PO** *1967*
Wotan	F. Frantz	G. London	T. Adam	D. Fischer-Dieskau
Fricka	I. Malaniuk	K. Flagstad	A. Burmeister	J. Veasey
Alberich	G. Neidlinger	G. Neidlinger	G. Neidlinger	Z. Kelemen
Loge	W. Windgassen	S. Svanholm	W. Windgassen	S. Stolze
Donner	A. Poell	E. Waechter	G. Nienstedt	R. Kerns
Froh	L. Fehenberger	W. Kmentt	E. Esser	D. Grobe
Mime	J. Patzak	E. Wohlfahrt	E. Wolfahrt	E. Wolfahrt
Fasolt	J. Greindl	W. Kreppel	M. Talvela	M. Talvela
Fafner	G. Frick	K. Boehme	K. Boehme	K. Ridderbusch
Freia	E. Grummer	C. Watson	A. Silja	S. Mangelsdorff
UK Record Number	RLS 702	414 101-1	6747 037	2740 145
UK Tape Number	–	414 101-4	–	–
UK CD Number	–	414 101-2	412 475-2	415 141-2
US Disc Number	–	414 101-1	–	2709 023
US Tape Number	–	414 101-4	–	–
US CD Number	–	414 101-2	–	415 141-2

Conductor	R. Goodall	P. Boulez	M. Janowski
Orchestra/Opera House	English National Opera	Bayreuth Festival	Dresden Opera
Date	*1974*	*1979/80*	*1981*
Wotan	N. Bailey	D. McIntyre	T. Adam
Fricka	K. Pring	H. Schwarz	Y. Minton
Alberich	D. Hammond-Stroud	H. Becht	S. Nimsgern
Loge	E. Belcourt	H. Zednik	P. Schreier
Donner	N. Welsby	M. Egel	K.H. Stryczek
Froh	R. Ferguson	S. Jerusalem	E. Buchner
Mime	G. Dempsey	H. Pampuch	C. Vogel
Fasolt	R. Lloyd	M. Salminen	R. Bracht
Fafner	C. Grant	F. Hübner	M. Salminen
Freia	L. McDonall	C. Reppel	M. Napier
UK Disc Number	SLS 5032	6769 079	301 137
UK Tape Number	TC SLS 5032	–	501 137
UK CD Number	–	–	610 058
US Disc Number	–	6769079	301 137
US Tape Number	–	–	501 137
US CD Number	–	–	610 058

Bibliography

Wagner wrote *Eine Mitteilung au meine Freunde* (A Communication to my Friends, 1851) as an introduction for them to the form of *The Ring*, and *Oper und Drama* (*Opera and Drama*, 1852) sets out these new theories of opera. Both essays are included in *The Complete Prose Works of Richard Wagner*, translated by W. Ashton Ellis, which, although neither accurate nor fluent, is the most widely available translation (London, 1892-99; reprinted 1972). Robert Hartford's chronicle of *Bayreuth: The Early Years* (London, 1980), and the eye-witness account of the stage rehearsals of the first Bayreuth Festival in *Wagner Rehearsing the 'Ring'* by Heinrich Porges (trans. R. Jacobs, Cambridge, 1983) give a picture of the first cycles. The two massive volumes of *Cosima Wagner's Diaries* (I, 1869-77; II, 1873-83) make astonishing reading because of their frankness and comphrensiveness (ed. Gregor-Dellin and Mack, trans. G. Skelton, London, 1978, 1980). Wagner's biography *My Life* trans. A. Gray, ed. M. Whittall, has been published by Cambridge (1983).

Among the numerous biographical and musicological accounts of Wagner, there are two short introductions: the Master Musicians volume by Barry Millington (London, 1984) and the New Grove volume by John Deathridge and Carl Dahlhaus (London, 1984). Martin Gregor-Dellin's *Richard Wagner, His Life, His Work, His Century* (London, 1983) is of interest despite its highly subjective standpoint but in translation is less than half the length of the original German. *I Saw the World End* by Deryck Cooke (Oxford, 1979) and *Wagner's 'Ring' and its Symbols* by Robert Donington (London, 1963) are brilliant and densely argued commentaries on the cycle. Carl Dahlhaus's perceptive *Musicdramas of Richard Wagner* (trans. M. Whittall, Cambridge, 1980) includes chapters on the cycle.

The Perfect Wagnerite by Bernard Shaw (London, 1898; New York, 1967) and *Wagner Nights* by Ernest Newman (London, 1949) are classic introductions to the cycle. The commentary by Paul Bekker in *Richard Wagner, His Life and Work* (trans. M. Bozman, New York, 1931, 1971) is still exceptionally rewarding. John Culshaw's account of recording the Decca *Ring* cycle is of interest to lovers of the score as well as record enthusiasts: *Ring Resounding* (London, 1967). *'The Ring': Anatomy of an Opera* by Stephen Fay and Roger Wood (London, 1984) is an exciting account of the preparation for the 1983 Bayreuth *Ring* cycle. For those interested in the staging of *The Ring*, Oswald Georg Bauer's study *Richard Wagner, The Stage Designs and Productions from the Premières to the Present* (Rizzoli, 1982) contains both accurate text and beautiful illustrations. Also beautifully illustrated is *Wagner, a documentary study* (ed. Barth, Mack and Voss, London, 1975) which in 1983 went into a second edition, in German only, much enlarged and updated.

Thomas Mann's *Pro and Contra Wagner* (trans. Allan Blunden, London, 1985) contains as its centrepiece his lecture 'The Sorrows and Grandeur of Richard Wagner'. Stewart Spencer and Barry Millington are currently working on a new critical edition of Wagner's letters.

Colette describes a visit to Bayreuth for a performance of *The Rhinegold* in *Claudine and Annie* (Penguin, 1972).